You Shall Not Condemn

You Shall Not Condemn

A Story of Faith and Advocacy on Death Row

JENNIFER M. McBRIDE

CASCADE *Books* · Eugene, Oregon

YOU SHALL NOT CONDEMN
A Story of Faith and Advocacy on Death Row

Cascade Books
An Imprint of Wipf and Stock Publishers
199 W. 8th Ave., Suite 3
Eugene, OR 97401

www.wipfandstock.com

PAPERBACK ISBN: 978-1-7252-6379-6
HARDCOVER ISBN: 978-1-7252-6373-4
EBOOK ISBN: 978-1-7252-6376-5

Cataloguing-in-Publication data:

Names: McBride, Jennifer M., author.

Title: You shall not condemn : a story of faith and advocacy on death row / Jennifer M. McBride.

Description: Eugene, OR: Cascade Books, 2022 | Includes bibliographical references.

Identifiers: ISBN 978-1-7252-6379-6 (paperback) | ISBN 978-1-7252-6373-4 (hardcover) | ISBN 978-1-7252-6376-5 (ebook)

Subjects: LCSH: Moltmann, Jürgen, 1926–. | Christianity and justice. | Church work with prisoners.

Classification: BS680.J8 M50 2022 (print) | BS680.J8 (ebook)

For Thomas

"Do not condemn."

LUKE 6:37

Table of Contents

Acknowledgments

KEY

WE NEVER KNOW HOW acts of faithfulness will unfold or where they will lead. I think of this often, mostly in relation to the prison theology program where I met Kelly Gissendaner. It was a program that Emory University ethicist Elizabeth Bounds and Georgia Department of Corrections chaplain Susan Bishop dreamed about for years and then established in 2008. Who would have known that a warden would break prison protocol and allow Kelly to enter the second cohort of students, even given her death row status, or that five years later a broad community of people connected to the theology program would play the leading role in an international advocacy movement on her behalf?

I also think of this in relation to the Project on Lived Theology, an institute launched by Charles Marsh at the University of Virginia, where I met and hosted German theologian Jürgen Moltmann while working there during graduate school. Who would have thought that five years later this internationally renowned theologian would be corresponding with Kelly and developing a friendship that would be definitive for her and central to our campaign? "Friendship" is an essential theological category for Moltmann (or "Jürgen" as he invited me to call him, since, as he told me, "my first name is not 'Professor'"). In friendship, Jürgen says, we experience a "broad space" in which we can expand. Sharing a circle of friendship with Kelly and Jürgen has had that expansive effect. It is hard to capture the vast gratitude and affection I feel for Jürgen as a result of my own conversion to hope and as a result of watching him love Kelly so well.

As I share in the Introduction, I am but one character in this story and the custodian of the letters between Jürgen and Kelly. There are a great number of people who played a significant role in Kelly's development and in the advocacy campaign, many of whom I know personally but some I only know, admiringly, from a distance. And there are many more people who participated in vigils and actions in Atlanta, around the country, and around the world, who go unnamed. I am grateful for Susan Casey, Kelly's primary appellate attorney, who made a point to get to know me early in my friendship with Kelly and who embraced those of us leading the advocacy campaign as partners in their work. I am grateful, too, for Robert Mc-Glasson, a good friend and death penalty lawyer who provided support and served as a consultant of sorts for our circle of advocates. I have enormous admiration for Kelly's entire legal team, including the late Patty Daniel, Lindsay Bennett, and Beth Wells. I am grateful for the circle of Kelly's close friends who accompanied her during her "death watch" visits, including Sally Purvis, Judy Wells, Amanda Peterson, Cathy Zappa, Della Bacote, Karen Miller, and the late Murphy Davis. I am grateful to have worked alongside and learned from the organizers of Kelly's advocacy campaign, including Letitia Campbell, Kimberly Jackson, the late Melissa Browning, Wes Browning, Jeania Ree Moore, Christina Conroy, Nikki Roberts, Rebecca Spurrier, Cassandra Henderson, Brendan Ozawa-de Silva, Steffen Lösel, Trina Jackson, Joe Wiinikka-Lydon, Brenna Lakeson, Kara Stephens, the "Struggle Sisters," and Don Plummer. Gratitude also goes to friends in the media who helped get Kelly's story out, including Mark Oppenheimer, David Cook, and Katia Hetter. I am grateful for religious leaders like Raphael Warnock of Ebenezer Baptist Church and Robert Wright, Bishop of the Episcopal Diocese of Atlanta, who used their large platforms to speak on Kelly's behalf at a press conference. And I am grateful for the constant faithfulness of communities like the Open Door, New Hope House, Georgians for Alternatives to the Death Penalty, the Diocese of Atlanta, and Central Presbyterian Church, all who take a stand each and every time a person is threatened by death in the state of Georgia.

When Kelly's clemency was denied I went to my dear friend Andrea White's home, where some of the people named above were gathered. With my head still swirling from the news, I asked why she and another friend of mine were there, and why she was hosting, since neither of them had been directly involved in the theology program at the prison. "We're here because of you," Andrea said. In those assertive and loving words, I experienced for myself the power of a movement built on networks of solidarity and friendship. In fact, old friends and colleagues from around the country and across the ocean reached out to see how they could help. Lauren Winner offered to draft the template that religion scholars could use as they crafted letters to the Parole Board, when I couldn't think clearly enough to write a polished version myself. Colleagues detoured from their syllabi and shared Kelly's story in their classrooms as the movement was unfolding. And colleagues and students at my own institution at the time supported me and held a prayer service before I traveled to Atlanta, including Chip Bouzard, Ramona Bouzard, Kit Kleinhans, Judith Jones, Brian Jones, Kuni Terasawa, Bonita Brock, Alex Thibodo, and Fatima Pai. I am grateful, too, for my brother and sister-in-law, David McBride and Lucy McBride, who provided me a home base while in Atlanta.

The entire book is a memorial to Kelly and a labor of love rooted in our friendship. I am grateful for the opportunity I have had to get to know her children, Kayla, Dakota, and Brandon, and to watch up close their remarkable tenacity and strength. Additionally, students in the prison theology program formed a supportive community with Kelly and one another and endured these events as they took place. No advocacy concerning prisons would be possible without the witness, leadership, and love of people who are surviving and have survived prison.

In the years since Kelly's execution, I have had the opportunity to share her story with a variety of groups. I am grateful for invitations from Aaron Conley, Minde Smyth, and the Denver Faith and Justice conference in November 2015; Charles Marsh and the Project on Lived Theology in December 2015; Nichole Flores, Nadia Boltz Weber, the late Rachel Held Evans, and the "Why Christian?" conference in September 2016; the Wild Goose Festival in July 2017 (where I presented with Nannette Banks); Charles Crawley, Intersections Interfaith Alliance of Iowa, and Coe College in February 2018; Ed Bacon and St. Luke's Episcopal Church in Atlanta in July 2019; and Jim Wright, Heather Keaney, and Westmont College in October 2019.

I am grateful for the colleagues and friends who have supported me during the writing process itself. McCormick Theological Seminary generously provided me with a six-month sabbatical to write this book. My colleague, Daniel Schipani, graciously covered my administrative responsibilities in the doctor of ministry office while I was gone, and the entire faculty at McCormick engaged the material at a scholarship lunch in one of our last in-person gatherings before the pandemic. A handful of close friends and colleagues have helped me process this story as I wrote and have offered constructive feedback on drafts: Mary Catherine Johnson, Mary Gage Davidson, Janel Kragt Bakker, Paul Lutter, Sarah Hedgis, and

Lori Hale. Jason Francisco professionally scanned the images used in the book. And many months prior, my parents Mary Jane McBride and John McBride lovingly transcribed the first draft of Jürgen and Kelly's correspondence. I am grateful, too, for the support of my colleague Henco Van Der Westhuizen and for the Historical and Constructive Theology Department at the University of the Free State, South Africa, where I was appointed a research fellow. I am fortunate to have been able to work with two of the great editors in the industry, Michael Thompson and Rodney Clapp, at Cascade Books.

This book is dedicated to my husband, Thomas Fabisiak. He was there in the circle of advocates at Andrea's house before I knew him well. He has read many drafts and helped me process the material on an almost daily basis. While running a higher education in prison program, he has modeled what it looks like to live a life free of condemnation, and in his everyday advocacy he embodies the hope at the heart of this book—the possibility of a new world. Our relationship has provided the healing I needed to face this task and has been a constant source of joy, wonder, and play as we look expectantly together to the *novum*, the new thing, promised to come.

Season after Pentecost, 2021

Introduction

"I LEARNED THAT I was already a practicing theologian even before I began my formal study of theology," Kelly Gissendaner wrote to me in August 2010. "The purpose of the classes was to articulate and seek some answers to questions I had consciously and unconsciously been struggling with my whole life."

At the time, Kelly was the only woman on Georgia's death row, until her execution in 2015. In January 2010, while incarcerated in a Georgia women's prison, Kelly had become a student in the Certificate in Theological Studies, a program developed by ethicist Elizabeth Bounds and chaplain Susan Bishop, housed at Emory University's Candler School of Theology, and co-sponsored by Candler and three other Protestant seminaries in Atlanta—Columbia Theological Seminary, McAfee School of Theology, and the Interdenominational Theological Center. The certificate was open to any incarcerated person who at least held a GED or a high school diploma, like Kelly, who had graduated in 1986 from North Gwinnet High School in Gainesville, Georgia and afterwards joined the army. After reading the work of German theologian Jürgen Moltmann in a theology foundations course that I taught at the prison, Kelly began a five-year correspondence with him. When she was denied clemency, a local and international advocacy movement arose that was rooted in her theological studies and friendship with Moltmann. The advocacy campaign challenged Christians who supported the death penalty to reexamine basic truths of Christian faith, including the possibility of redemption, the nature of forgiveness, and the triumph of life over death. As it was unfolding, the story of transformation changed people's minds, not only about Kelly's case, but also about the death penalty itself. This book retells that story in the service of abolition, highlighting the role theological studies played in her faith development and in advocacy efforts on her behalf. It also showcases some of her own

theological writing, including the correspondence between Kelly and Jürgen Moltmann, one of the most internationally respected and widely read
theologians of the twentieth and twenty-first centuries.

I refer to this account of faith and advocacy as a "theological narrative" since it is a story bursting with theological meaning and consequence.
The story reveals that theology has social and political implications, which
are, at times, as serious as life and death. As Kelly's theology professor and
former program director of the certificate at the prison, my role during the
advocacy campaign was to tell Kelly's story through a theological lens in
print for outlets like CNN.com and *The New York Times* and in interviews
with outlets ranging from CNN to the Christian Broadcasting Network.
My role, then, was to be a public theologian, to demand that people think
theologically about what was happening, especially because one of the
main groups of people we were trying to reach were Christians who supported the death penalty in Georgia and beyond. Part of our advocacy work
was helping people enter the narrative and see the unfolding events as an
invitation to dwell within the larger story the Bible tells. In this regard, we
might refer to the story not only as a theological narrative but as a kind
of theological drama, a theater of divine and human action. The theological drama played out, for example, in the letters between one of the most
widely read theologians of the modern era and a lone woman on death row,
as she worked out her "faith seeking understanding" (to use the phrase of
the eleventh-century church father Saint Anselm). The theological drama
was seen at the clemency hearing in which the Board of Pardons and Paroles cast aside principles of church-state separation and appealed to Jesus'
cross to validate the death penalty, a scene that perhaps can only happen in
what novelist Flannery O'Connor called "the Christ-haunted South." The
theological drama was seen in an advocacy movement trying to practice
the this-worldly character of Christian hope in the face of seemingly inevitable death. It was seen in the striking parallels between the biblical story of
the passion of Christ and an execution in the United States.

The story may also be described as "theological advocacy" not only
because the primary activists in the #KellyOnMyMind movement and the
primary advocates at her clemency hearing were theological educators,
seminarians, and pastors, but also because Kelly asked that her story be told
and retold for the sake of others on death row. The story then is not simply
about something that happened in the past. It has present power. Kelly's
intent in asking me to continue to tell the story long after she was gone, and

her intent in entrusting me with the letters, was that her story and witness would be a form of advocacy for other men and women on death row.

Moreover, the correspondence between Kelly Gissendaner and Jürgen Moltmann belongs within the genre of theological letters from prison akin to the published correspondence between pastor-theologian and Nazi resister Dietrich Bonhoeffer and his best friend, Eberhard Bethge. The power and beauty of the correspondence between Kelly and Professor Moltmann lies, in part, in the fact that they occupied radically different social locations yet built a friendship through a shared journey of theological reflection. This dynamic story of faith and advocacy as well as the model of friendship across difference and the content of the letters all offer a theological foundation for the abolition of the death penalty.

The theological narrative is told in Part One, "Lived Theology on Death Row," and is divided into two sections. "Building Up Ruins" focuses primarily on Kelly's transformation and the practice of her faith. In it, I make use of some of Kelly's own writing, of a theological text we studied together that frames the section, and of anecdotes from our friendship. This section also draws significantly on the many voices and testimonies presented in her clemency application, written by her lawyers Susan Casey and Lindsay Bennett, and submitted to the Board of Pardons and Paroles before her clemency hearing. Like Kelly, at the end of the appeal process most individuals on death row apply for clemency—the process by which someone convicted of a crime petitions for a pardon or reduced sentence. And most, like Kelly, ask for their sentences to be commuted from death to life without parole. While the majority of death penalty states give the governor power to grant clemency, in Georgia, the Board of Pardons and Paroles serves as the sole acting authority, and, as political appointees of the governor, there are no set qualifications to serve on the board. The clemency application is a unique document because it is written for the particular audience of the board, who hold certain assumptions about the legitimacy of the death penalty and the fairness of the clemency process, which I do not share. Still, any of us who wrote for it had to play into these assumptions to a certain extent. Despite its original audience, this document became an invaluable resource for telling Kelly's story here, because it allowed me to draw from a wide variety of people who offer a detailed and authentic picture of who Kelly was in prison. Many of these people had known Kelly before I met her and had interacted with her daily. The testimonies drawn from the clemency application also highlight the kind of substantive content the board received about Kelly before they made their decision.

The section "Hope Is Protest" then focuses on our advocacy efforts on Kelly's behalf. The section draws on my experiences during the advocacy campaign and on my theological reflection during and after the events. This section also introduces the reader to Jürgen Moltmann, in part through his autobiography *A Broad Place*. It illustrates the similarities between Professor Moltmann and Kelly's journeys of faith, namely, that each were shaped by their imprisonment and conversion to hope as they built from the ruins of their past. The section also highlights letters from religion scholars and religious leaders who advocated for Kelly as their theological colleague. Their individual letters, when taken as a whole, cover most of what would be addressed in a unit on capital punishment in a college or seminary course on Christian ethics. In this way, the letters contribute to the telling of this story as theological narrative.

Part Two, "Letters and Papers from Prison: Correspondence with Jürgen Moltmann," publishes the letters between Kelly and Professor Moltmann. The letters begin in July 2010 and end with Kelly's execution in September 2015. All of her letters to Professor Moltmann are here, including some of the theological writing she sent him. But the prison lost the last batch of letters from Professor Moltmann to Kelly that she had asked to be sent home to her stepmother—an example of the heart-wrenching losses that happen in prison when people and their handful of personal items are treated as if they hold little to no value. Because Professor Moltmann either handwrote or typed his letters on a typewriter, there are no copies of his last letters, written between the summer of 2013 and the summer of 2015. We do have his final letter to Kelly, which was resent by fax on the day of her execution and read to her over the phone to ensure she received it. Part Two also publishes pictures of Kelly that were intentionally used during our advocacy campaign. We sought, and succeeded in part, to gradually replace the image used by various media outlets, namely her Department of Corrections mug shot, with pictures that captured Kelly's personality and spirit. Many of these pictures were taken at the graduation ceremony of the theology certificate program.

Part Three, "The Dawning of a New Day," addresses the devastation of Kelly's execution and answers a question posed to Professor Moltmann: How are we to understand hope in light of her death? The chapter examines a dominant theological position about the cross that hinders this-worldly

hope and asks Christians to reconsider how we speak about Jesus' own execution and God's role in it. The chapter then turns to Moltmann's theology
of hope to offer a constructive answer to the question posed to him. His
understanding of hope inspires resistance to the death penalty and related
powers and offers a theological foundation for abolition. The chapter ends
with practical ways that Christians and congregations who are born to a
living hope may enter this work.

I have told Kelly's story as a theological narrative and emphasized the
theological foundations of abolition not only because the story lends itself
so well to this, but also to honor Kelly, who wanted it to be told this way.
Although earlier in her sentence Kelly had subscribed to a Bible program
through the mail, which increased her familiarity with Scripture, it was the
interdisciplinary, academic, theological education and learning community
she gained in the certificate program that ignited her spirit. "While I was in
the theology courses, I was the most excited about life and the most positive
I'd been since coming to prison," she wrote to me. "I finally had something
that challenged my mind, spirit, and soul. I learned more . . . than I ever
thought was possible in a short amount of time. The more I learned in the
theology courses, the more I wanted to learn. I began to live, sleep, eat, and
breathe theology."

Although I knew Kelly wanted me to write this book, it took some
time to begin working on it. At times it felt like it wasn't my story to tell. I
am only one character in the story, and so it has been important to me to
bring in as many voices as possible from Kelly's deep and broad community. In this way, just as the writers of the four Gospels tell the story of Jesus
each through a specific theological lens, making particular points, so, too,
am I aware that I am telling this story from my particular angle, and there
are other people who lived this who also have stories to tell.

To be honest, at times, it has felt like a burden to be entrusted with this
task. It has necessitated time for healing, or more accurately, patience, on
my part for the deserts in my life to become springs of water, as the psalmist says, for the parts of my life that hungered to be filled with good things
that have, in turn, nourished me and strengthened me for this work. I am
grateful for the benefit of hindsight that I have gained in the last six years.
The distance has allowed me to reflect on what I wasn't able to understand
in the present, because of the demands and intensity of the moment, surreal
situations I was navigating for the first time that were affecting me in ways
I wasn't fully aware. This is the gift Kelly gave me when she asked me to

write this book. Although she probably didn't realize it at the time, she was giving me the gift of healing through the process of writing. The writing has enabled me to process what happened that just wasn't possible at the time, or quite frankly in the years ever since, until I immersed myself in the story one more time and met her again in it. So, while this story is for Kelly and a fulfillment of a promise to her, I now see that it is also her gift to me.

The clarity I have gained from writing this book, be it a sharper view of Kelly's unique gifts and personhood, or a deeper understanding of the theological truths we studied together, all point to the unfinished nature of our friendship and the unfinished nature of Kelly's own ministry and development. Kelly's story illustrates that the death penalty amounts to a wastefulness of life, a mechanism through which society discards the good creation God made and continues to remake. Southern religious folk artist and Baptist minister Howard Finster depicts this well in the admonishment he painted on a reclaimed trash can: "God sent not his son to condem. Jesus did not condem. You should not condem."[1] Understanding himself as a man of visions, Finster turned swamp land in Georgia into a "Paradise Garden" filled with art mostly made from metal scraps and inscribed with lines from Scripture. His vibrant trash can is but one witness to the beauty of creation and re-creation, as well as a critique of our inclination to throw away people and things that hold promise and value. Kelly's story exemplifies this truth, both the witness and the critique, as it makes clear that Jesus' straightforward command, "Do not condemn," is the heart of the gospel and the key to a new world.

---

1. For a color image of Howard Finster's "Waste Can," see https://high.org/collections /waste-can/ and https://kaopweb.com/2015/03/13/the-high-decorative-arts-design -permanent-collection/.

Howard Finster, "Waste Can," 1979.

Part 1

Lived Theology on Death Row

THE FIRST STORY OF murder that the Bible tells comes right on the heels of the Genesis account of humanity's creation and fall: "Cain said to his brother Abel, 'Let us go out to the field.' And when they were in the field, Cain rose up against his brother Abel, and killed him. Then the Lord said to Cain, 'Where is your brother Abel?' He said, 'I do not know; am I my brother's keeper?'" God responds with words that at once convey the severity of the act and demand justice: "What have you done? Listen; your brother's blood is crying out to me from the ground!" (Gen 4:8–10).

The murder of Douglas Gissendaner has striking similarity to this brief biblical account. Like Abel, Doug was a good person, "a loving and generous husband and father."[1] As Kelly Gissendaner's lover Greg Owen was leading her husband Doug into the woods at knifepoint, carrying out an act she set in motion, Kelly was with friends at a bar.[2] Later, she reported Doug missing with the same words of deception used by Cain: "*I do not know* where Doug is," she would repeat to her children, family and friends, co-workers, the media, and search teams. Years later, when she shared with me more about the crime, I asked why she had done it. The phrase originally

---

1. Casey and Bennett, "Clemency Application," 3.

2. Kelly set in motion the murder of her husband by initially proposing the idea to Greg Owen and sticking with the idea after their decision was made. These are the actions that make the Cain and Abel story so relevant from a moral perspective. From a legal perspective, however, there are important distinctions between her actions and those of Greg Owen, which should have made a difference in her sentencing, not only during her trial, but also during the clemency hearing (see Casey and Bennett, "Clemency Application," 49–52 and "Emergency Application," 10–12).

1

meant to deceive had now become honest reflection on an act without justi-fication: "I do not know," she said, shaking her head remorsefully.

In the story of Cain and Abel, "the true nature of killing is revealed," writes scholar Lee Griffith, namely, that every intentional act of killing another human being is indefensible and "devoid of any sense." "To all of God's questions"—Why are you angry? Where is your brother? What have you done?—"Cain can only answer, 'I do not know.'"[3] Kelly's inability to make sense of the crime, even as she would take full responsibility for her role in it, is an ethical posture in line with the truth the story of Cain reveals: Any purported reason for taking human life would ultimately be unsound. Kelly's admission, "I do not know," is at once a confession of her own grave sin and a challenge against any form of killing (personal or institutional) that claims to know—that claims to be reasonable or justified. Every act of intentional killing strikes at the heart of creation, degrading the life in which we all share, the life that God brought into being and called "very good" (Gen 1:31). It is not only the blood of Cain or the life force of Doug Gissendaner that cries out to God from the ground, then. The ground of our collective being cries out when blood is intentionally shed.[4]

What is most striking about the story of Cain and Abel is God's re-sponse to the collective cry of creation when life is taken. God responds to Abel's murder with loving concern not only for the victim but also for the perpetrator. When the Lord says to Cain, "And now you are cursed from the ground, which has opened its mouth to receive your brother's blood from your hand; when you till the ground, it will no longer yield to you its strength; you will be a fugitive and wanderer on the earth," Cain cries out that this is more than he can bear. For he, too, is now susceptible to violence and harm. "Today you have driven me away from the soil, and I shall be hidden from your face; I shall be a fugitive and wanderer on the earth, and anyone who meets me may kill me," he exclaims. "Not so!" the Lord retorts. Whoever intends to kill Cain will answer to God, for judgment belongs to God alone (Rom 12:17–19). In the face of retributive killing, God inter-venes, stopping the cycle of violence. God puts "a mark" on Cain so that "no one" who comes upon him "would kill him." Cain goes away and settles in the land of Nod, east of Eden (Gen 4:15–16).

The mark on Cain not only reveals that God's justice is rooted in the preservation and restoration of life, it also exposes the inadequacy of

3. Griffith, *Fall of the Prison*, 87.

4. Griffith, *Fall of the Prison*, 87.

human forms of justice that perpetuate violence or harm. Griffith writes, "Cain is guilty as sin, and yet in violation of all human 'justice,' God protects him. Even before we are told of God's establishment of the law, we are told of God's mercy in the face of lawlessness."[5] In the absence of the law, what we have in the story of Cain, then, is not simply the forgiveness of individual sin or the wiping clean of a legal or moral ledger. Rather, the power of mercy and forgiveness is its ability to intervene in cycles of violence, to stop retribution and further harm, and in its place establish a social reality that benefits not only the offender but the communal whole.

It is important to say now—at the start of a story of an execution—that God's mark on Cain parallels God's intervention on the cross. Instead of continuing the cycle of violence perpetrated by the political and religious powers, Jesus exposes their violence as he suffers crucifixion. He then returns as the Resurrected One to those who condemned him to death, and instead of continuing the cycle, instead of making them victims of condemnation and retaliatory violence, he offers them forgiveness, reconciliation, the opportunity to repent and become co-laborers in the kingdom of God.[6]

In God's mark on Cain, we are shown nothing less than the heart of the gospel—the good news of God's reign, a reign characterized by human interdependence and responsibility, repair and repentance, healing and restoration, surprise and possibility, and the transformation and newness of life. The good news is the triumph of life over the powers of death. "Here already in Genesis 4, the history of God's relationship with humankind is summarized," writes Griffith. "As we persist in choosing death, God chooses life on our behalf. As we deny responsibility to care for sisters and brothers ('Am I my brother's keeper?'), God intervenes to show us how. . . . Cain is a marked man. We would mark him for death. God marks him for life."[7]

Like Cain's, Kelly's crime is that she did not affirm life, the sacred and particular life of Douglas Gissendaner, a good man and a father to her children. The scandal of the gospel is this: Even given that severe and painful reality, God affirmed Kelly's life and called her forth into fullness of life. God affirms all of life.

5. Griffith, *Fall of the Prison*, 88.

6. Williams, *Resurrection*, 1–5.

7. Griffith, *Fall of the Prison*, 88.

Building Up Ruins

I met Kelly in January 2010 in a nondescript classroom at Metro State Prison for Women near Atlanta. She arrived for class beaming with excitement about the journey she was about to begin—participation in a yearlong academic theology program jointly sponsored by four Atlanta seminaries. Since she had been sentenced to the death penalty and lived in solitary confinement, Kelly was eager to share community with others, if only one morning a week. And she was grateful for the opportunity to explore the Bible and theology in a rigorous manner that would nurture and deepen her devotional life. That image of her on the first day of class remains vivid to me because it captured the core of who Kelly was, who she had become— someone full of contagious joy and gratitude, open to others and to new experiences for growth and ministry.

Kelly's process of transformation began during the first few years of her prison sentence, following her 1998 conviction for planning the murder of her husband. A team of dedicated spiritual mentors—prison chaplaincy staff, chaplain volunteers, and a United Church of Christ pastor, who would become Kelly's primary pastoral counselor—started visiting her and initiated a series of difficult, yet compassionate, conversations that urged her toward courageous self-reflection. A core group of these ministers accompanied Kelly for the entirety of her sentence, for almost seventeen years. For me, their collective description of her change brings to mind the conversion of Paul in the book of Acts, not in terms of the immediacy of the conversion (there was no sudden flash or blinding light for Kelly), but in terms of the totality of the transformation—a conversion that, for Paul, turned a persecutor and murderer of Christians into their apostle.

"When Ms. Gissendaner first entered the prison system she was a very closed and self-centered person with little insight," writes Susan Bishop, a prison chaplain serving in the system for thirty years. "I have seen her evolve into a person who is very concerned for others. . . . The spiritual transformation and depth of faith that Ms. Gissendaner demonstrates and practices is a deep and sincere expression of a personal relationship with God."[8]

"When I first met Kelly [in July 1999], she was an angry woman," echoes Kelly's pastoral counselor, Sally Purvis. "I am not breaking pastoral confidence to say that she grew up in an angry and often violent environment since that is public record. And she had absorbed much of her upbringing. Early in our relationship, I spent a lot of time helping her to

8. Casey and Bennett, "Clemency Application," 5.

understand, that yes, it's true, life isn't fair, and all of the emotional and spiritual energy she was using being angry . . . was just wasted. She gradually took responsibility . . . and she started to look hard at what she had done. She realized over time that her real work . . . was to look hard at her own soul and make peace—with God, with the world, and with herself."[9]

"Initially, she could not face the gravity of her role in taking her husband's life and the pain and destruction his murder wrought on their children and extended family," her appeals attorney, Susan Casey, writes in her clemency application. "Overwhelmed, Kelly hid from what she had done, maintaining a tough and arrogant persona." Eventually, with the support of her mentors, Kelly was able to face herself and "confront the terrible truth. What Kelly saw when she looked in the mirror was a selfish and bitter person who 'no longer valued life.' Experiencing God's forgiveness was nothing short of transformative. Gradually, the layers of self-serving behavior and self-loathing thinking began to peel away."[10]

The pastoral and legal team's commitment to Kelly provided steady, ongoing love that fostered change. So, by the time I met Kelly in 2010, she had already undergone "a complete metamorphism," to use the words of volunteer minister Dottie Benson. "The butterfly had left the cocoon."[11]

In the academic theology program, Kelly learned to love God with her mind in a way that strengthened her already active devotional life. She asked honest questions about her relationship to God, others, and the world. She read Scripture and grappled with centuries-old theological questions. She began to develop her authentic theological voice in the midst of this work. "From the start of the theology class I felt this hunger," she said in her 2011 graduation speech. "I became so hungry for theology, and what all the classes had to offer, you could call me a glutton," she added with signature wit.

In the certificate program, the Bible was read in light of the experiences and hopes of incarcerated students. Together, they came to see that their biblical and theological reflections could be a gift to the wider church as well as to their community in prison. By studying historical and contemporary Christian thinkers, they entered the conversations that make the Christian tradition dynamic. They learned that courageous questioning is

9. Casey and Bennett, "Clemency Application," 5–6.

10. Casey and Bennett, "Clemency Application," 3–6.

11. Casey and Bennett, "Clemency Application," 53 (verb tense changed from original).

not antithetical to faith in Jesus but central to it, as captured in St. Anselm's famous phrase, "faith seeking understanding." In an Old Testament course, for example, incarcerated students wrote their own lament Psalms and risked honest words boldly directed at God. In a womanist theology course, they focused on unnamed women in Scripture and explored the texts from their perspectives, granting the biblical women voice even as they granted themselves the same. In a homiletics course they wrote sermons, some of which were later preached in the prison chapel during a worship service. In a pastoral care course, they learned theories of human development and practical skills for spiritual care that deepened their ministries inside the prison. In a course on German pastor-theologian and Nazi resister Dietrich Bonhoeffer, students wrote theological letters from prison, as he did, sharing what they learned with family and friends. The courses not only catered to the students' individual growth but also tried to meet some of their basic social needs, like the need for community or a sense of belonging and for opportunities to express agency. As the students grew together in intellectual freedom, they also grew in an interrelated psychological freedom. They internalized the truth of their created and personal worth as they grappled with the course material and discovered new capacities and insights that most of the students did not know they had. In turn, they were better equipped to survive prison and resist its dehumanizing character. They had more resources to help them heal from their pasts and reflect on their lives in honest and nuanced ways.

My relationship with Kelly began in the classroom as I got to know her and other incarcerated women not only as students but also as kindred spirits who, like me, were wrestling with some of life's most urgent questions. And it only deepened six months into the year when her situation changed with the arrival of a new warden. In her graduation speech Kelly described this moment: "There came a time when . . . my worst fears became my reality—I was pulled from the courses. I was taken from my theological community. Being pulled from the program devastated me as badly as if someone had just told me one of my appeals had been turned down." The previous warden who made Kelly's participation possible had taken a risk by breaking prison protocol, allowing her to be in community with other incarcerated students four hours a week. But the new warden had no reason to remove Kelly from her peers beyond her death row status, making her decision seem calculated and cruel. "Since I couldn't go to the theology class," Kelly said in her speech, "the instructors came to me. . . .

That gate . . . was meant to keep everyone and everything separated from me. But that gate couldn't keep out the knowledge that I was so hungry for, nor friendship and community. And it sure couldn't keep out God." With the warden's decision, Kelly lost the rare opportunity to gather with peers for lengthy conversation, energized by critical reflection and an openness to new ideas—difficult work made easier in a classroom community built on trust. What she gained was something the other theology students already had (in the form of study hall, which Kelly was not allowed to attend)—the opportunity to have one-on-one time with individual professors.

This change afforded us the chance to have two hours of conversation every Friday afternoon, sometimes through the bars of her cell and other times around a table in an adjoining room. It gave me the rare opportunity to be invited into Kelly's living space and gave us room for the deepening of friendship, which is not always possible in the classroom alone. During this time our friendship grew to encompass all aspects of our lives, be it sharing some small joy or pleasure, like when Kelly was allowed to mow the grass one summer day, or venting about some frustrating experience one of us recently had, like Kelly dealing with an especially loud dorm: "Between the women yelling back and forth and these huge fans running, it will drive you crazy, in my case, crazier ☺," she wrote to me during those first months of shared time together. The authenticity of our friendship included the vulnerability of friendship, the intimate knowledge friends gain about one another over time that leads to inside jokes or banter that, every once in a while, may hit a sensitive nerve; the intimate knowledge that allows friends to care for one another in unexpectedly thoughtful ways, like when Kelly told me visitation started an hour later than it did because she knew how much I loved my sleep. When I moved from Georgia to Iowa to serve on the faculty at a college there, Kelly and I stayed in close contact. I saw her, along with the rest of my former students in prison, during summer and holiday breaks. During those visits, Kelly and I continued to have hours of one-on-one time together, a blend of informal conversation and formal study.

In one of the texts we studied together, former Archbishop of Canterbury Rowan Williams argues that new life—resurrected life—must be built upon the ruins of our past. If Ms. Dottie's imagery of a butterfly leaving its cocoon accurately portrays the colossal change in Kelly (the butterfly has long been used as a symbol of the resurrection, a vivid image of the "new creation" Paul proclaims in his second letter to the Corinthians), then Rowan Williams's writing helped us articulate the proper relationship between the old that has gone and the new that has come (2 Cor 5:17). This relationship has ethical consequence, especially when the old includes an irreparable act that leaves so much destruction and pain in its wake.

In a sermon based on Isaiah 61:4, "They shall build up the ancient ruins, they shall raise up the former devastations," Williams writes that the new creation—the new age of God's reign—"is not a general utopia in which all that has gone before is simply canceled." Instead, living by the power of the resurrection necessitates "going back to the ruins of the past . . . and building there, with the help of God, a city which is new but which still stands on the same earth as the old."[12] Whether understood as a renewed person, or, as Paul intended, a new age (the kingdom of God breaking into this old world), new creation is not an erasure of what came before. An act of negation would only disregard and further harm the victim Doug, who must be remembered in anticipation of God's future coming. For God does not forget victims of violence but, in accordance with the eschatological promise, brings them with him to the "new earth" where God's creative justice "is at home" (2 Pet 3:13).[13] Instead of erasure or reversal, risen life is recapitulation—the gathering together of the moments and memories of our past to be "taken up" and "healed in a new age."[14] And so "restoration can only begin *here*," on the ash heap, in the wreckage.[15] This understanding of risen life affirms what we already know, if we are honest, what we already experience about other people and within ourselves: "that I am one person, one person with one life, a seamless coat, every moment sewn into every other."[16] Williams argues that the Apostle Paul exemplifies what it means to hold together the old and new self. He affirms this unity "in joy and amazement, time and again, recollecting that he was a persecutor, with martyrs' blood on his hands, and yet knowing that from that persecutor God made an apostle. For Paul, this is the most extreme and unexpected work of the risen Christ."[17]

---

12. Williams, *Ray of Darkness*, 64.

13. Moltmann, Reformation Day Lecture, "Sun of Righteousness, Arise!," given at Emory the same weekend as his visit with Kelly at the prison. This lecture draws on his then-recently published book, *Sun of Righteousness, Arise!*

14. Williams, *Ray of Darkness*, 66.

15. Williams, *Ray of Darkness*, 64.

16. Williams, *Ray of Darkness*, 65.

17. Williams, *Ray of Darkness*, 67.

The Gospel narratives make this unity clear in the apparition stories when Jesus appears to the disciples in risen form. Not only does Jesus' new resurrected body bear the old marks of crucifixion, in that body Jesus leads his disciples "with their memories of terror and betrayal and shame" back to the beginning of their stories. "It is on that ground or nowhere that restoration begins."[18] Most poignant in this regard is the story of Peter. Peter's threefold confession of love and threefold acceptance of Jesus' call builds upon his threefold denial. Likewise, the place where Jesus calls Peter into his pastoral responsibilities is reminiscent of the place where Peter denied him. Williams writes, "An unobtrusive but haunting detail—there is a 'fire of coals' burning on the shore, just as there was in the High Priest's courtyard (the only two occasions when the expression appears in the gospel). Peter . . . must smell again the sour scent of his betrayal in the drifting smoke of the fire. On that foundation rests his future, his pastoral authority."[19] Williams concludes,

> There is no shattering conversion that blots out the shame and wretchedness of the past; no, [the disciples] are led through it again by the hand of Jesus, gentle and relentless. Here I called you, here I broke bread with you, here you betrayed me; and here I still stand with you, calling you and breaking bread with you again and giving you a destiny in my love. . . .
> Risen life in and with Christ is now, entirely fresh, full of what we could have never foreseen or planned, yet it is built from the bricks and mortar, messy and unlovely, of our past. . . . *Our* earth, *our* dull and stained lives, these are the living stones of God's new Jerusalem.[20]

As I reflect on who I knew Kelly to be, and listen to the many voices recorded in the testimonies that comprise her clemency application, I see that she lived this truth—that risen life is built from the ruins of the past—long before we read Williams's sermon together.

Building from the ruins necessitates being able to acknowledge and name the devastation, which is another way of saying that it necessitates confession of sin. Because the call to build up ruins is not abstract but precise—Christ's "light must make its way into every corner"—the call requires

18. Williams, *Ray of Darkness*, 65.

19. Williams, *Ray of Darkness*, 66.

20. Williams, *Ray of Darkness*, 66–67.

that we confront and examine the details of our lives.[21] Doing so makes confession of sin not a manifestation of "cheap grace," to use Dietrich Bonhoeffer's helpful term, but of "costly grace." Bonhoeffer defines cheap grace as merely a general recognition of one's sinfulness and of God's forgiveness that avoids confessing specific sin and, in turn, prevents one from responding with concrete acts of repentance. Dealing in generalities amounts to a "cheap cover-up" for one's sins. When we hide the details of our lives from ourselves, others, and God, we reveal, as Bonhoeffer says, that we have no "desire to be set free."[22] But costly grace follows Christ into the hidden corners, leading us to continuous growth and repair. Costly grace goes back to the ruin and raises up former devastations.

In her clemency application, Kelly offers her concrete confession before the Board of Pardons and Paroles:

> It is impossible to put into words the overwhelming sorrow and remorse I feel for my involvement in the murder of my husband, Douglas Gissendaner. Doug was a wonderful person and a loving and generous husband and father. Because of my actions, our children lost their beloved father, the Gissendaner family lost their beloved son, brother, and uncle, and our community lost one of its finest citizens. I wish I could truly express how sorry I am for what I did, but there is just no way to capture the depth of my sorrow and regret. I would change everything if I could.
>
> There are no excuses for what I did. I am fully responsible for my role in my husband's murder. I became so self-centered and bitter about my life and who I had become, that I lost all judgment. I will never understand how I let myself fall into such evil, but I have learned first-hand that no one, not even me, is beyond redemption through God's grace and mercy.[23]

Kelly's acknowledgment of her sin bore out daily, as volunteer chaplain Della Bacote observed, through a repentance that took the form of "a profound sense of responsibility to help others and contribute to her community within the correctional institution."[24] Her acts of responsible repentance happened, in the words of Chaplain Bishop, "not occasionally but consistently," most poignantly in her ministry to other residents of the prison, especially those in lockdown near her cell, and in her participation

21. Williams, *Ray of Darkness*, 66.
22. Bonhoeffer, *Discipleship*, 43–44.
23. Casey and Bennett, "Clemency Application," 3.
24. Casey and Bennett, "Clemency Application," 6.

in prison prevention programs for so-called "at-risk" youth.[25] In response
to the outpouring of observations about Kelly's conduct in prison from correctional officers, prison administrators, and prison residents, Susan Casey
writes in the clemency application addressed to the Parole Board,

> The above observations offer a compelling look at Kelly Gissen-
> daner's daily life . . . and comment on her routine, her demeanor,
> and her impact on those around her. This contextual view dem-
> onstrates its authenticity: an [incarcerated person] cannot falsely
> maintain such good behavior and goodwill toward others over the
> sustained and lengthy period of time these individuals were with
> Kelly—every hour, every day, every year for 16 years.[26]

Kelly's everyday speech also demonstrated the consistency of her confession about whom she had been. Theology instructor Rachelle Green, who
taught a course on the social and theological influence of women in history,
shared this: "When reading those women's stories and hearing how they
took stands for justice, Kelly often told me how her life choices did the
opposite. She was so open and honest in her regret and her desire for other
women to be more like the women we were studying: courageous enough
to think about the wellbeing of others when they decided to act."[27] And
when, like any of us, she stumbled in the daily course of her life, when she
"had minor run-ins with the correctional staff," for example, she admitted
when she was "in the wrong and offered an apology," observed one prison
lieutenant.[28]

Since Kelly's ruins included her crime as well as her past bitterness
and resignation, building from that particular wreckage meant that she was
"uniquely positioned" to minister to other incarcerated people "in a way
that few others could," as they struggled "to find their identity in the face of
their offenses" and the barrenness of prison life.[29] As former warden Vanessa
O'Donnell observed, Kelly "can provide hope to the most desperate [wom-
en in prison] in a manner that no one else could possibly understand."[30] This

25. Casey and Bennett, "Clemency Application," 21.

26. Casey and Bennett, "Clemency Application," 28.

27. Casey and Bennett, "Clemency Application," 41.

28. Casey and Bennett, "Clemency Application," 16.

29. Casey and Bennett, "Clemency Application," 7.

30. Casey and Bennett, "Clemency Application," 22–23. Throughout the quotations,
I have replaced state language for incarcerated persons with language that reminds us of
their humanity.

was her practice and her intent. In her clemency statement, Kelly writes, "Over the past 14 years, I've come to know that I have a great responsibility to live my life and serve others as best I can to honor Doug's memory and the person he was. I strive every day to 'pay it forward,' to try to make a positive difference in the world. I try to use the life and light God has given me to help those around me in whatever ways I can."[31]

Kelly did this most consistently through direct encouragement, namely by initiating conversation with women placed in lockdown near her, speaking through the ventilation and plumbing systems that connected their cells. Although this was a practice that risked disciplinary action, it became clear to officers across the ranks that Kelly's words had great positive effect: "She helped make the [dorm] less disruptive and more tolerable," writes one officer. She was a "peacemaker" and "made the job safer for me and my staff," writes another.[32] "I watched Kelly reach out to scared, terrified young women and assure them that they could survive and . . . find peace. The other [residents of the prison] really listen to Kelly when they will not listen to anyone else."[33]

Nikki Roberts addressed Kelly's influence in a powerful testimony captured on video during advocacy efforts on Kelly's behalf. "The first time I met Kelly," says Nikki,

> I was on suicide watch at Metro State Prison in the lockdown unit, where they sort of carried me in. I made enough noise to awaken people miles away. Certainly, the cell next to me was aware. In that cell was Kelly Renee Gissendaner, who heard me screaming and wishing death upon myself—I wanted to die. I had cut my wrists . . . in fact I had almost done damage to a vein. And Kelly, not knowing me at the time personally, spoke to me through an air vent and said, "*Stop* giving up your power. *Don't* give up your power. You *will* live, and you are going to do great things. Don't die; don't you dare say you want to die. Do you know these people will take you off the count and keep going?" And I realized that, later on seeing death, that it's a reality, and in the system it's a matter of numbers. She told me to do something with myself.
>
> When you are faced with, first off incarceration, but definitely a long sentence—I had no parole, and so in 2004 I was pretty much told I'll see you in 2014. It seemed very dark. But Kelly stirred in

---

31. Casey and Bennett, "Clemency Application," 11.

32. Casey and Bennett, "Clemency Application," 14, 22.

33. Casey and Bennett, "Clemency Application," 19.

me a new sight that allowed me to see that I had a worthiness. I engaged myself in many different positive outlets and became a peer mentor at the same facility that I had been considered to be a disciplinary problem. At a place and at a time where I had once been hopeless, I had hope. Her positive suggestions, even just for me, gave life to me. Now the way that I have been able to replicate positivity in my life should speak volumes [to who Kelly is] . . . She's being judged for taking one life, but she is not being granted mercy for giving so much life to others.[34]

Sierra Burns, another woman whom Kelly ministered to while on her hall, similarly shares,

One day I was sitting in my room and thought that that was it for me, right as I was about to do something I would've never had the chance to regret, Kelly . . . asked . . . was I alright. . . . I believe Kelly was my guardian angel that day, my voice of reason, and I needed that. . . . She made me look at my life in a whole new way . . . Kelly showed me that even when faced with indescribable circumstances you still have so much to live for. So many people and things to love, to love about life. Every day is a gift and it is to be cherished.[35]

Sierra ends her written testimony with a turn of phrase reminiscent of a title of one of Jürgen Moltmann's books that Kelly was reading—*In the End—the Beginning: A Life of Hope*—language she must have heard from Kelly, who, as one theology instructor observed, would share what she was learning "with other women who ended up in lock-down near her premises."[36] Sierra says, "I have a newfound hope, this is just my end to a new beginning, and honestly it took Kelly for me to realize that."[37]

Kelly's peacemaking practice of sitting on the floor, up against the wall, head tilted toward the vent—or sometimes standing up straight, bellowing spiritual guidance through the corridor toward a cell down the hall—became a fixture of her ministry to others, both to the individuals residing in lockdown and to the correctional officers charged with monitoring that space. As it turned out, that practice also had "a positive ripple effect," to use the words of one officer, who wrote that she heard many women on the

34. "Nikki's Story."
35. Casey and Bennett, "Clemency Application," 26–27.
36. Casey and Bennett, "Clemency Application," 41.
37. Casey and Bennett, "Clemency Application," 26.

compound "talk about Kelly's example far from the lockdown area."[38] Ex-emplifying this expansive reach, Tracy Harley, who was incarcerated with Kelly, writes,

> I have had the opportunity to assist with the orientation process for new intakes during my sentence. Over the years I have used Kelly's positive influence on my life as an example for and an inspiration to those coming into the system desperate for some sign of hope to help them hold on, instead of giving up. They see that even in the darkest circumstances, one can find light and do positive things. These ladies can start to believe in themselves and their chance for a future, which is something many of them never had or lost upon becoming incarcerated.[39]

Echoing this sentiment, theology student Kimberly Pugh writes, "Kelly made me realize that I can't give up on myself when everyone else has already given up on you . . . I vow . . . to one day give to someone . . . what Kelly Gissendaner has instilled in me: a Fire and Determination to be the best I can be no matter where I am."[40]

Kelly's influence across the prison was clear to me before I met her. One of the first things I learned about Kelly from theology students in the inaugural cohort was how they would engage with one another when she was being moved across the compound. The residents of the prison were ordered to turn their backs to her when she walked by, and neither party was allowed to speak. It was always a spectacle, as Kelly, considered the highest security threat at the prison because of her death row status, would be the only person handcuffed and shackled—her feet and hands connected to her midsection by chains that weighed her down, slowed her pace, and made noise as they clanked together. When Kelly walked by a large group of people, the turning of their bodies, one right after the other, looked like a human wave. Many theology students, who had never met Kelly personally, spoke of their decision early on not to comply with this particular prison rule. Instead, they would face her and look her in the eye, or slightly turn away but rotate their heads across their shoulders, and offer a simple, "Hello, Kelly." Kelly would respond with a smile, nod, or word of greeting. These small but significant acts of solidarity contributed to Kelly's inner strength, in turn empowering her service to others.

38. Casey and Bennett, "Clemency Application," 20.
39. Casey and Bennett, "Clemency Application," 26.
40. Casey and Bennett, "Clemency Application," 27–28.

Kelly was determined to share what she learned in the theology program with other people, both inside and outside prison walls. Referring to Kelly's final project—a ninety-day devotional journal that she entitled *A Journey of Hope*—theology instructor Hannah Ingram writes:

> Kelly committed herself to creating a devotional from what she had learned because she wanted to impact others. She inspired me with . . . her dedication to open herself up to others so that they might be encouraged. She would frequently share her thoughts and writings with me and other instructors eager for their feedback and collaboration. She wanted so badly for her work to mean something to people other than herself. And it did.[41]

In the preface to the devotional, Kelly speaks directly of this desire: "I hope the words on the pages that follow touch you, teach you, and open your eyes to a new way of looking at God and a prisoner."

> Over the course of the Certificate in Theological Studies Program and through much reading and studying, I've learned that the Bible is not a book of saints, but of sinners and prisoners. God's word is full of very real women and men; it tells of their failures, struggles, and sorrows. But it is also a story of their victories—won through the power of the God of Israel revealed in Jesus the Christ. . . .
>
> As I began to read the Bible, I discovered that it was full of people like me; who had made big mistakes, caused a lot of pain, had been forgiven and healed. After I committed my life to Christ, (for real this time!), I saw the same healing process slowly take place in me. I had been bruised and battered inside. Have you? Jesus Christ restored me; I am no longer bent on destruction, but filled with new life and love.

The devotional opens with a prayer "For Today" that reveals that new life on death row was for Kelly both a gift and hard won. The prayer is based on her favorite Bible verse, initially brought to her attention through the writings of Billy Neal Moore, who was sentenced to Georgia's death row until the Parole Board commuted his sentence. The prayer, written in more formal language than Kelly actually prayed, is an example of her working out her evolving theological and pastoral voice, at least on paper.

41. Casey and Bennett, "Clemency Application," 38.

Please stand on this Scripture daily with me:

Psalm 118:17,

"I shall not die, but live, and declare the works of the Lord"

O God:
Give me strength to live another day;
Let me not turn coward before its difficulties or prove faithless to its
duties;
Let me not lose faith in other people;
Keep me sweet and sound of heart, in spite of ingratitude, treachery or
meanness;
Preserve me from minding little stings or giving them;
Help me to keep my heart clean, and to live honestly and fearlessly,
So that no outward failure can dishearten me or take away the joy of
conscious integrity;
Open wide the eyes of my soul that I may see God in all things;
Grant me this day some new vision of Your truth;
Inspire me with the Spirit of joy and gladness;
And make me a cup of strength to suffering souls;
In the name of the Strong Deliverer,
Our only Lord and Savior,
Jesus the Christ. AMEN.

Because Kelly saw her primary role as an encourager, her devotional entries took that tone. She wrote in a didactic style, outward facing, offering hope to others, instead of writing *cor curvum in se*, with a heart turned in upon itself, as one consumed with her own tortured ego. Her focus was always on the life that had been built from the ruins, as exemplified in the devotional's opening words, "Regardless of where you are today, or what you are facing, keep faith and hope alive, and recognize that God is bigger than your mountain or issues. Regardless of one's lot in life, things can change for the better. Remember, where there is life, there is hope—and where there is hope, there is life!"

In her speaking and in her writing, Kelly was an encourager who knew, as Rowan Williams says, that her pastoral authority rested on where she had been and what she had fostered since then—a love for life built on the ruins of death. Indeed, for the individuals incarcerated with her, her love for life served as an affirmation of their worth and as a model of resistance to the destructive powers that characterize the prison system.

It is important to pause and clearly state that Kelly's time in prison—her ministry and even her "good behavior"—was characterized by resistance.

16

During it, she affirmed her life and worth over against the carceral forces that dehumanized her and condemned her to death. The story told in her clemency application for the Parole Board did not, of course, depict her life this way, as one of resistance. (Rather, it took the form of a classic "personal redemption" narrative.) We strategically highlighted this sin-and-redemption narrative in our advocacy efforts as we called on Christians to recognize the authenticity of Kelly's transformation and denounce her execution. And we strategically petitioned the Board of Pardons and Paroles to embrace this narrative as a Department of Corrections success story.

But here's the tension. (Stories of sin and redemption,) at least within dominant forms of Western Christianity, tend to strip the good news proclamation of its social, political, and cosmic power. In turn, many Christians presume concepts like sin and redemption apply only to our individual and interpersonal lives. Such a reading falsely turns the gospel into a morality tale, in which transformed people like Kelly deserve reward for finding redemption while those who remain unchanged deserve punishment and death. In contrast to an individualistic understanding of the faith, Kelly's daily prayer from the Psalm, "I shall not die, but live, and declare the works of the Lord," was at once personal and political. The prayer was not only for herself but was a prayer, she told me, for all men and women on death row: It was a prayer for abolition. The transformation Kelly sought for herself and others was simultaneously personal and structural—the transformation of one's inner spirit from despair to hope alongside the transformation of societal systems that give reason for despair.

In other words, Kelly's experience of restoration happened in spite of, not because of, the carceral system. The ruins Kelly continuously built from *included* her daily experience of incarceration, for the prison is an engine of trauma, enacting violence on bodies and souls.[42]

In a poem entitled "Fearful Encounters," Kelly speaks of the traumatic and monstrous weight of the powers of death that surround her. In an imaginative reflection on Matthew 6:9–13, where Jesus teaches the disciples to pray for God's kingdom to come on earth and triumph over rulers and political powers that contradict God's intent, Kelly personifies her fears as visitors at the prison. "I peeked into the room," she writes. "It was quite crowded. Many people were checking their watches as if they were

42. An upsurge of scholarship in the last decade (statistical studies, critical analysis, and personal testimony) has taught us that the prison is an engine of trauma. See, for example, Baranyi et al., "Prevalence of Posttraumatic Stress Disorder"; and Liem and Kunst, "Post-incarceration Syndrome."

expecting someone. I took a deep breath before opening the door. I'm the one they're expecting." It was a diverse group, "but I recognized them immediately. They were my worst fears." One by one, Kelly asks who they are.

> "I'm your fear of being abandoned," says one man as he adjusts his tie. "You never know who might walk out of your life."
>
> "I'm your fear of dying," says a well-dressed woman in a proud tone of voice. "I've been with you ever since you were placed on death row." She gestures to another woman sitting behind her, "She reports to me. She's your fear of suffering."
>
> "I work really hard and put in long hours. I think I deserve a raise." I had to agree with her. Since my federal appeals had started, she'd been paying me a visit first thing in the morning and last thing at night. I certainly couldn't accuse her of slacking off.
>
> "I'm one of your main fears," says a man with his hand held high, looming tall over the rest. "I underpin all the others. Without me the rest would be nothing." He paused and then delivered the punch line, "I'm your fear that the promises of Christ are false. I'm your fear that when you die you will confront total nothingness."
>
> A hush fell over the room. Everyone looked at me, but I was too stunned to reply. I couldn't deny what he'd said. Didn't Christ say over and over, "Fear not," and "Don't let your heart be troubled"? Wasn't he always saying, "Peace be with you"?

Kelly's imaginative reflection then draws on a powerful passage in Romans 8, in which Paul sets the work of Christ and the Spirit over against earthly rulers and political powers that condemn human beings. Paul writes, "If God is for us who is against us? . . . Who is to condemn?" (v. 31, 34). With a close paraphrase of Paul, Kelly concludes, "For nothing can separate you from the love of Christ, no ruler or power or anything else in all creation."

Kelly then notices a man "with big soulful eyes" sitting by himself in a corner. "Which fear are you?" she asks.

> "I'm not a fear," he said quietly, "I sneaked into the meeting out of curiosity. I represent hundreds of others who aren't here right now. I stand for all the prayers still being said for you by your friends, church communities, family, fellow prisoners, and theology course teachers."

He reached out his hand and Kelly grasped it firmly.

> As his fingers intertwined with mine, I felt my anxiety starting to ebb. But then suddenly there was an ugly sound of snarling and growling. Looking up I saw the fears rising from their seats.

Horrified, I realized they were heading straight for us. Mouth dry, heart pounding, I did the only thing I knew how to do. I tightened my grip on the gentle guy's hand and closed my eyes. Then I began to pray aloud: "Our Father who art in heaven, hallowed be thy name. Thy kingdom come, thy will be done on earth . . ."[43]

By praying that God's kingdom come and triumph over the terrifying powers of abandonment, suffering, and death—by praying that God's will be done *on earth*—Kelly countered her death row condemnation. As the poem shows, it was her active resistance to carceral forces of isolation, disintegrative shame, and bodily threat that sustained her in prison. It was her active resistance, empowered by the Spirit of God and the communities of faith and solidarity that supported her, that fueled her repair and life-giving ministry to others. Through this ministry she proclaimed that they, too, could find strength to affirm their worth and the goodness of life despite the material conditions and systemic forces working against them.

It is remarkable that within a context that deliberately restricts agency, Kelly found ways, and took whatever opportunity presented itself, to try to live a renewed life based on the Genesis truth that we are each other's keeper. And she did so while living in solitary confinement, detained inside her cell twenty-three hours a day. Early in her sentence, in 2001, she began participating in prison prevention programs, speaking to youth who toured her cell, a practice she continued for well over a decade. When Kelly told me about her involvement with these "scared straight" programs, I was concerned about their hyper-individualistic approach—an approach that defines our entire prison system, a system that disregards societal forces like institutionalized racism and endemic poverty that drive mass incarceration and even the death penalty itself. But Kelly saw her participation as a way to build up ruins, to convey to these students the simple truth she learned too late, that our actions have consequence and may do irreparable harm. As her clemency application states,

> Kelly's desire to interact with the children is born of a real desire to help them learn how to thrive in the world. . . . Perhaps it is her straight-up no nonsense manner and her willingness to be honest about the crime she committed that causes the children to listen to her. Most impressive to [program leader] Marc Easley was how Kelly's straight talking down to earth style resonated with the students and left lasting impressions.

43. Gissendaner, unpublished poem, in the author's possession, 2010.

19

A middle school teacher who accompanied students on the prison tours writes that Kelly helped the students "have respect for themselves."

> Kelly admitted that she didn't have all the answers, but in order for students to avoid being channeled into the system they needed to look toward what is needed to become successful in society and find ways to . . . get involved in systems that support that. In addition, she further encouraged them to . . . look for ways to make things better, such as finding constructive ways to deal with issues without blaming parents, teachers, peers, or family members. She cautioned that blaming makes us feel good because then it isn't our problem—it is someone else's fault. . . . She encouraged us all to step up and work together to make a positive change.[44]

High school teacher Lisa Logan reminisced that after Kelly had spoken to one group of students and the last one left the area, Kelly turned to her and asked searchingly, "Do you think I made a difference?" Some of the students who had been in the program submitted testimonies for Kelly's clemency hearing, assuring her she had: "I want Ms. Kelly to know that her work from prison is not in vain. We are representing her great influence in the free world by turning our lives around, volunteering our time, and paying it forward every opportunity we get."[45] As her lawyer Susan Casey summarizes, "Kelly knows that she cannot take away the pain she has caused to so many. But through her work with these children, . . . she prays that she may be able to save some other family the pain she has caused her own."[46]

In her clemency application, Kelly speaks to this pain, especially the pain she brought on her children, who were twelve, seven, and five at the time of the crime:

> I pray every day for our children, Brandon, Kayla, and Cody, and for the entire Gissendaner family. I know that I have caused them unbearable and irreversible pain. I pray that God gives them the freedom to live above the darkness and despair I have caused in their lives. I pray that they can find some measure of peace and healing. I hold them close to my heart.[47]

Kelly's time with the students, it seems to me, served in part as a way for her to begin the long journey of attending to the ruins that were the most

44. Casey and Bennett, "Clemency Application," 33.
45. Casey and Bennett, "Clemency Application," 34, 32.
46. Casey and Bennett, "Clemency Application," 35.
47. Casey and Bennett, "Clemency Application," 44.

devastating to her—the damaged relationship with her children, especially before reconciliation with them became a possibility and reality. Her engagement with the youth who visited her cell exemplified the truth that risen life built from the ruins is full of surprise—as Rowan Williams says, "full of what we could have never foreseen or planned."[48] Another surprise of her risen life is the poignant fact that, after interacting with Kelly in lockdown, many residents of the prison started to refer to her, lovingly, as "Mama Kelly."

One such woman was Keisha Rhodes, who, like other young women entering the prison, was placed in a segregated cell on the lockdown unit. Keisha writes,

> I'm 18 years old. Kelly has really made a great impact on my life. She shows me a love that my mother didn't show me . . . She is a very good influence on my sister and the rest of the juveniles that's housed here. When I wanted to give up, she wouldn't let me, she treated me just like I was her own child. So I started calling her Mama Kelly. I would come up and see her, we would talk about my goals and how to . . . get over the hard obstacles in my life. When I would see my Mama Kelly she always made me smile. And I know God put her in my life for a reason.[49]

Theology student Valerie Carter says that she has "met several young women" who refer to Kelly this way. Valerie writes, "She always has words of encouragement and wisdom to offer other women who are going through nearly as much as she is. Kelly really cares for the women she mentors."[50] Recalling one woman "who had significant problems adjusting" to prison and wanted to stay in the lockdown unit "close to Kelly" instead of being released to general population, Lieutenant Marion Williams likewise observes, "Kelly was like a caring mother to many."[51]

Just as there is tension when referring to Kelly's story as a sin-and-redemption narrative, because it risks turning her story into a morality tale that validates a framework of reward and punishment, there is a similar tension when speaking about Kelly as mother, since notions about motherhood impact how women are punished. In general, men receive harsher sentences than women, but women can be punished more harshly when

48. Williams, *Ray of Darkness*, 67.

49. Casey and Bennett, "Clemency Application," 25.

50. Casey and Bennett, "Clemency Application," 25.

51. Casey and Bennett, "Clemency Application," 17.

they are viewed as distortions of ideal womanhood or as betraying traditional gender roles, especially in the South.[52] This is seen, for example, in
the presumption of guilt aimed at poor women and women of color when
babies are stillborn or when children die unexpectedly.[53] In Kelly's case, it
is seen in the fact that her co-defendant, who admitted to personally carrying out the murder and planned the majority of the details of the attack,
was judged less culpable than Kelly and given a sentence of life with the
possibility of parole.[54] When I speak of Kelly as mother, then, I do so not to
reinforce gendered understandings of sin and redemption but to honor her
commitments and appreciate the surprises that punctuated her risen life.

Kelly's care extended beyond maternal words of wisdom to include
basic provisions like food. Georgia prisons do not serve lunch on weekends
and holidays, so in order to avoid hunger, people imprisoned there have to
have money on their accounts to buy food from the commissary. Whenever
there was someone on her hall that didn't have any, Kelly would share hers.
One officer observes, "There are a lot [of people] that go hungry. . . . I know
one of [the individuals with a life sentence] told me herself that Kelly saved
her life when she first came to prison. She had no outside support. . . . Kelly
bought her a cup and bowl and sent them to her. She began eating and
for the first time started talking."[55] Directing resources meant for her to
others was common practice for Kelly, whether those resources met material or spiritual needs. Volunteer chaplain Bruce Janzen recalled a time, for
example, that Kelly turned away his pastoral visit and directed him to her
neighbor instead, who was grieving the loss of a loved one and needed care.
Kelly's watchful eye was attuned to the needs of others and even included
new officers who were still learning the job. One officer writes,

> Fortunately, Kelly did not choose to take advantage of my lack of
> knowledge. . . . Instead, if she saw I was forgetting to do something
> or failed to do something she would tell me, "Mrs. Roberts you
> might want to do that a different way or talk to a superior officer
> about that situation." When I would check with my superior officer
> about it, Kelly was always right. She kept me out of a lot of trouble
> and reduced the risk of any potential problems on the range. If she

52. Holland and Prohaska, "Gender Effects Across Place."

53. Bryan Stevenson, *Just Mercy*, chapter 12; Gibson, "Evil Women Hypothesis," para.
5.

54. See Casey and Bennett, "Clemency Application," 49–52 and "Emergency Application," 10–12.

55. Casey and Bennett, "Clemency Application," 19–20.

did hear of other . . . problems that might be rising she would also let me know so that in many instances I could stop things before they happened."[56]

What did not come out in Officer Roberts's comments—but that I can hear as plain as day—was the playful, yet respectful, tone with which Kelly likely delivered the line, "Umm, Mrs. Roberts you might want to do that a different way." Kelly's play and sense of humor disarmed situations and created possibilities, in this case, allowing her to risk advising an officer who could use the help. Her playfulness was central to her personality and a key part of her ministry, although it only came up a couple of times in the clemency testimonies. One volunteer wrote about a time she was visiting women in lockdown and didn't know that Kelly lived down the hall. When she was ready to leave, the officer that escorted her "was laughing" as she walked toward her "and shared how uplifted she felt every time she spoke to Kelly."[57] In another testimony, a resident of the prison captured Kelly's classic humor when she wrote, "Walking past SMU where Kelly is housed, [individuals] would yell and say 'Hello Kelly' and identify themselves." Kelly would peek out her small window and respond, "Are you behaving yourself? I don't want to hear you are in lockdown! Don't let me catch you up here. I miss you but I don't want to see you."[58] I imagine most of us appealing to the Parole Board were not explicit about Kelly's humor because we instinctively knew that, although it was a gift to particular officers and staff who interacted with her, her playfulness was another way her life proved to be one of resistance to the prison system itself.

Humor played a significant role in Kelly's ability to live with some peace and express compassion toward others in SMU, the Security Management Unit that includes lockdown cells for solitary confinement. While constant noise is characteristic of the entire prison compound, the lockdown unit can get especially loud and chaotic. It serves as a holding ground—the "jail" in prison vernacular—for individuals deemed "behavioral problems" by the administration. This population includes a high percentage of people with severe mental illness, who are disproportionately represented in solitary confinement and pose the greatest risk of suicide. While the vast majority of women in prison battle with at least mild depression as they endure the trauma of prison, one study offers a conservative estimate that at least 15

56. Casey and Bennett, "Clemency Application," 20–21.
57. Casey and Bennett, "Clemency Application," 8.
58. Casey and Bennett, "Clemency Application," 23.

percent of women in state prisons suffer from severe mental illness, defined as schizophrenia, bipolar disorder, brief psychotic disorder, schizoaffective disorder, and major depression.[59]

In her clemency testimony, Lieutenant Williams writes of two women with severe mental illness who were decompensating in lockdown. She describes a scene I had heard from Kelly in some form or another multiple times: "they would kick, hit, spit, . . . bite, scream at the top of their lungs, cuss the staff, and smear feces all over their cells."[60] I would be wide-eyed as I took in the details of the stories Kelly shared, which not only conveyed the massive failure of our society to provide dignified care, but also put into sharp relief the living conditions Kelly endured daily. Yet she told these stories about life in her dorm with humor, not a humor that poked fun at particular individuals, but a humor that mirrored the playfulness with which she would engage other people in prison with her. "Most of the time the ladies would listen to Kelly . . . because she had been a friend to them," writes Lieutenant Williams. "Sometimes they would yell back [at her]," Williams continues, and then, with words that could have been spoken directly by Kelly as she told me the story herself, the lieutenant writes, "but by the time the lights went out they would be saying" in an entrusting and sweet-tempered voice, "we're sorry and we love you Kelly."[61] Had Kelly been telling the story, she would have delivered that line with a soft and gracious laugh.

In the clemency application one officer wrote admiringly that she did not know how Kelly did it, namely, how she could talk to people being held in lockdown and "calm them down."[62] I have come to see that Kelly's secret power was precisely her playfulness. Kelly knew that people tend to respond to a playful tone, especially when it conveys empathy and expresses curiosity about the other person. Playfulness communicates that you don't take the person's behavior in the moment too seriously, that you know it is not the sum total of their personality or personhood. Humor suggests that you are not put off by a particular behavior, or if you are put off, you are not going to let it define the other person in your eyes. Play conveys that you are not intimidated but interested and that you want to know more. Because of this dynamic, playfulness creates attachment and fosters growth in the

59. "Serious Mental Illness Prevalence in Jails and Prisons," para. 4.
60. Casey and Bennett, "Clemency Application," 17.
61. Casey and Bennett, "Clemency Application," 17.
62. Casey and Bennett, "Clemency Application," 18.

other person, as it creates space for vulnerability without judgment. This broad space—an image the Old Testament uses for salvation and healing—allows the other person, in turn, to be open to themselves, to face their own weaknesses and limits with gentleness and grace. An open, playful stance reassures another person that they cannot mess up with you, and, even more, it creates opportunity for spontaneity, for the other person to surprise herself or others. What's equally true about humor is that it is not only other-affirming but self-affirming. By using humor, Kelly maintained control over how she responded to terrible situations. She then continued to practice playfulness as she would process these interactions through stories that provided comic relief.

I have seen this kind of humor in some of the best pastors I have known, who use playfulness as a way of accepting people for who they are, of even loving the things that are challenging about them. It's a pastoral skill that people in ministry like Kelly develop and hone. It is also a trauma-informed practice, incorporated, for example, into parenting methods taught to adoptive families.[63] Kelly was not trained in trauma-informed ministry or parenting techniques, but she did know trauma. And she intuitively leaned into play for her own restoration and healing.

Through this healing, Kelly gained a lightness—a gentle and loving perspective on her own life—that she then extended to others. Theology instructor Cathy Zappa observes insightfully that with her sense of humor, Kelly "tried to soften the trauma of it all," not only for herself but also for those of us who visited her, and even for the officers charged with monitoring her every move.[64] When forced by prison protocol to take a shower in full view of an officer, she would often sing Michael Jackson's chorus, "I always feel like somebody's watching me. (Can I have my privacy?), uh-oh-oh." When she would enter a visitation room handcuffed and shackled, she would hold out her arms as the officer reached for the keys, and in a cheerful voice ask, "Do you like my jewelry?" Through that humor she re-established a sense of dignity for herself while also ministering to her family and friends, helping us be more relaxed in an inherently tense situation.

Kelly's playfulness was a mark of resiliency. Through her play she demonstrated that it is okay to feel good—to laugh and be lighthearted—even in the midst of oppression. Through play, she stood up for normal life in the inherently abnormal and humorless situation of incarceration. In this way,

63. See, for example, Golding and Hughes, *Creating Loving Attachments*.

64. Cathy Zappa, unpublished memorial comments, in the author's possession, 2015.

her playfulness was an expression of risen life, of the new that stands on the same earth as the old. It was an inbreaking of new creation.

I did not always have this ministerial insight when relating with Kelly—that lightheartedness was a way of dealing with what was otherwise somber and severe. I carry this regret, that I couldn't always mirror back to her what she reflected for others: a lightness of being in that weighty place. I wish I could tell her now that I better understand that the humor was not simply a part of her personality but a pastoral skill, at first hard won as a trauma survivor and then developed and refined. I wish I could tell her that my healing in the last few years, from my own particular pain and from the indirect trauma of the execution, has opened up deeper reservoirs of playfulness in me that, following her lead, I want to develop and hone. I don't know why, but I have always felt more comfortable with humor once the seriousness of the situation was directly acknowledged or addressed. Theology instructor Sarah Hedgis tells me that this, too, is a pastoral quality—to hold space for solemnity. Through it, I let Kelly know that I took her and her work seriously, something I know she sought that was easy to give.

 Kelly could hold at once both gravity and play. Theology student Iyabo Onipede captures well her ability to do this when she writes, "Kelly was always joyful and would laugh at jokes. She was more serious in the theology classes, but even there, she was always encouraging to the women."[65] Or as longtime volunteer Karen Miller similarly writes, "Kelly was eager to share good news about her children along with sharing the not so good news . . . when her appeals had been denied."[66] This ability to simultaneously hold competing experiences exemplifies what Bonhoeffer calls the multidimensional or polyphonic character of life. It is a rare ability, he argues, a mark of the spiritually mature. In 1944, writing to his best friend from a Berlin prison during an air raid, Bonhoeffer says,

> I often notice [here] how few people there are who can harbor many different things at the same time. When bombers come, they are nothing but fear itself; when there's something good to eat, nothing but greed itself. . . . They are missing out on the fullness of life and on the wholeness of their own existence. . . . We fear—(I've just been interrupted again by the siren, so I am sitting outdoors enjoying the sun)—for our lives, but at the same time we must think thoughts that are much more important to us than our

65. Casey and Bennett, "Clemency Application," 24.
66. Casey and Bennett, "Clemency Application," 8.

lives. . . . Life isn't pushed back into a single dimension, but is kept multidimensional, polyphonic (May 29, 1944).[67]

Kelly's spiritual capacity to hold together discordant melodies nourished her hope.

The moment that best captures, for me, a shared experience of gravity and play was when Kelly and I celebrated what the Open Door Community cleverly termed a "Vending Machine Eucharist." As a Protestant community grafted into the Catholic Worker movement, the Open Door was an intentionally interracial, residential, activist and worshipping community in Atlanta, that had been engaged in anti-death penalty work for over thirty years. From its start, founders Murphy Davis and Ed Loring also provided emotional and spiritual support for the appellate attorneys they got to know during death row visits and vigils, a rare show of Christian solidarity with lawyers dedicated to this work.[68]

At the Open Door Community, rolls of quarters took on sacramental value because they were the means through which Community members would break bread with the men they visited on death row. For years during worship, I had heard of these daylong visits and the power of the shared meal, understood as an extension of Sunday's Eucharist. On an almost weekly basis, during the prayers of the people, Community members would reflect on the details of the visit they made the day before. So, when Kelly wrote to me, "Don't forget the quarters," after I had moved away and was planning one of many return visits, it was only natural that I would hear it as an invitation to eucharistic celebration.

Although the majority of my time with Kelly would continue under the auspices of the theology program, every once in awhile, for various bureaucratic reasons, we would set up a "special visit" instead. Our meeting space had already changed from her cell, where we discussed theology on opposite sides of an iron cage, to a small room located off the large visitation area, accessible through two mechanically locked doors. Special visits gave Kelly and me the opportunity to share a meal, whatever we could cobble together from the vending machines that lined the back of the visitation room, something that program volunteers like me were otherwise prohibited from doing.

67. Bonhoeffer, *Letters and Papers from Prison* (DBWE), 404–5.

68. Christians tend to be the staunchest proponents of the death penalty, believing (incorrectly, this book intends to show) that the biblical witness supports it. For more on the Open Door Community, see McBride, *Radical Discipleship*.

Perhaps only inside a Georgia state prison do Big Az Bubba Twin Cheeseburgers become the real presence of Christ, but that was exactly what Kelly sent me off to buy, along with a bag of Cheetos, a twenty-ounce bottle of Diet Coke, and animal cracker cookies—sixteen quarters for the burger, four for the chips, eight for the Coke, and six more for the cookies. I opened the burger's plastic wrap, stuck it in a microwave that must have been the first model of its kind, turned the timer knob, and watched it sputter and shake. With an armful of food, I was buzzed back through the metal doors, the elements tumbling onto the short stool-like table between us. With smiles and a few laughs, Kelly and I acknowledged the humorous, holy act in which we were about to participate.

Empowered with authority conferred on me by the Open Door, I, a layperson, fumbled through the pages of Scripture until I came upon the appropriate Gospel text. "When it was evening, Jesus took his place among the twelve. While they were eating, he took the loaf of bread, and after blessing it he broke it, gave it to the disciples and said, 'Take, eat; this is my body.'" I paused and held the Big Az burgers up to the heavens. Replacing the burgers with the Diet Coke, I continued, "Then he took the cup, and after giving thanks he gave it to them, saying, 'Drink from it all of you, for this is the blood of the covenant, which is poured out for many for the forgiveness of sins'" (Matt 26:20–28).

We ate, drank, and caught up on each other's lives, enveloped by this sacrament. The little visitation room had already become sacred space for Kelly and me by virtue of the hours we shared there together. Our companionship was already eucharistic: "Where two or three are gathered in my name, I am there among them," says Jesus (Matt 18:20). The benefit of this conscious celebration, though, was an increase in faith, since faith comes from hearing the word proclaimed *pro nobis*—for us. As we celebrated the Eucharist with seriousness and play, we received God's word and lived into the polyphony of life. In that one unifying word of forgiveness and healing, the life of this death row prisoner and my own were bound together in the flesh of the incarnate God—in the comic materiality of a Big Az burger. There, in that burger and Coke, Jesus made himself present to us.

As the presence of Christ, the Eucharist meal is God's vision of justice, a vision that insists that forgiveness, repair, and healing are fundamental features of God's earthly reign. In this way, the Eucharist meal makes claims about the nature of reality itself. As we saw in the opening story of Cain, forgiveness is a power that establishes justice by interrupting cycles of violence and harm. In turn, it makes way for God's kingdom come, for the possibility of new relationships, like Kelly's and mine, or restored relationships, like Kelly's with her children.

As the material and communal character of this feast makes clear, the promise of God's reign is this-worldly and politically concrete. Through its celebration, the kingdom of God presses in and reveals that if the Eucharist is an accurate expression of God's justice and intent, then the death penalty is not. The Eucharist is God's definitive proclamation of forgiveness, but, in the words of Martin Luther King, "capital punishment is society's final assertion that it will not forgive."[69]

Only the most erratic thinking, then, could hold together the politics of this feast with the politics of state execution. Through eucharistic vision, punishment by death is exposed as a lie that counters the truth and validity of God's reign. The Eucharist announces that things are not as they must be—a new world has come. The reality of the new world being *here*, in *this* sacramental feast, creates the pressure Jesus displays in his first public address: "The time has come," Jesus says and the Eucharist shouts, "for captives to be released!" (Luke 4:16–21).

While the Eucharist is itself a political act, the eucharistic vision finds public expression through solidarity with those whom society condemns. The visitation room where Kelly and I met became overtly political space through the Eucharist meal, as the solidarity Paul proclaims in Galatians 3:28—in Christ there is neither prisoner nor free—was made real. Our eucharistic solidarity in the prison was, in that sense, a fulfillment of Jesus' liberating presence, even as it was also only a foretaste of a more holistic unity in which all things that separate us, like prison walls and sentences of death, will disappear. Whether consciously practiced or understood later as eucharistic celebration, the shared meal at prison visitation made manifest both the promise and present reality of God's reign.[70]

The eucharistic cup that Kelly and I shared followed me back to Iowa, this time as an expression of Kelly's solidarity and friendship with me. I had just returned from Atlanta, where I spent the holidays with family and friends, a much needed escape from the isolation and loneliness I felt in the Midwest. On a cold and dark late January evening, I gathered up the mail that had accumulated while I was gone and scattered it across the kitchen

69. King Jr., *Strength to Love*, 34.

70. A version of the vending machine Eucharist section was published in McBride, *Radical Discipleship*, 109–10, 112–14.

counter. There in the midst of junk mail and bills was a six-inch box and, in it, a pink and white coffee mug with large magnolia blossoms—a gift from Kelly.

Sending gifts from prison is an almost impossible task, out of reach for most incarcerated persons, who, at best, might be able to salvage and reuse a card they had previously received. To send a gift, Kelly would first have to ask a family member to use the money normally reserved for her for the purchase. She would then have to recruit a family member or friend to make the order and send it on. In one sense, I was accustomed to Kelly's gift-giving, which often took the form of coordinating a birthday card or framed handmade plaque signed by the theology class and presented to me at the prison, or that might take the form of a small item inserted with a letter, like the colored-pencil drawing she sketched for me on a white handkerchief one time. Perhaps because of the timing, having just returned to a place that was hard for me to be; perhaps because it had traveled so far; perhaps because it was such a generous gift from someone who had few resources and decided to spend them on me—that cup became a source of strength, reminding me of her friendship and the eucharistic presence of God.

I am embarrassed to admit that I was thrown off, though, by the writing on the mug. The mug had the look of an item one might find in a Christian bookstore, like a pillow or plate, inscribed with a Bible verse or inspirational message. The words were so flippant that they seemed to me to be an affront to the gravity of Kelly's own prayers. "God answers all prayers," the mug reads, "Sometimes He says 'Yes,' sometimes He says 'No,'"—and then in big letters—"sometimes He says, 'You've got to be kidding!'" But Kelly thought it was hilarious, I know, because she let out one of her big laughs when I thanked her in person the next time I saw her. What I now see is that the writing on that mug was, for Kelly, an affirmation: Just as she was playful with others—accepting, curious, not put off—God was playful with her.

Kelly's practice of play extended to her children, who share her robust sense of humor. Yet their mutual playfulness was not simply an expression of a shared family trait but was a visible sign of a reconciliation that had been hard-won. As lawyer Susan Casey narrates in the clemency application, "Criminal violence by one family member against another presents a uniquely difficult situation for healing," because "the loss is compounded by . . . simultaneous betrayal."[71] Casey writes,

> As the children grew into adulthood, all of them have experienced anger and bitterness toward their mother, leading each to cut off contact with her for varying periods of time. Kelly has done her best during those times to give them whatever space they needed, and to refrain from pressuring them to visit or re-establish contact, while also continuing to let them know by mail or occasional phone calls that she loves them deeply and unconditionally.[72]

After a year went by with no contact, Kelly suggested that she and her children participate in a "victim-offender dialogue," a restorative justice practice attentive to the needs of victims of crime. Those needs commonly include the opportunity to ask questions about the crime that only the one who has done the harm can answer, as well as the opportunity to share the raw truth about the effect the crime has had on their lives. The ability to tell one's story helps the one who has been harmed better integrate the experience into their lives, and creates a situation in which the one who has done the harm must confront the consequences of the crime in painful detail. All of these acts of truth-telling pave the emotional and psychological ground for accountability and healing.[73] As the clemency application states, "Although Kayla was wary at first, she agreed to go forward because she wanted answers from her mom concerning her dad's death. When she saw that her mother was truthfully answering those questions and putting forth the effort to mend their relationship, she realized that she wanted to try to have a relationship with her again."[74]

In a video made during advocacy efforts on Kelly's behalf, Kayla speaks in tender detail about the nature of their loss: "My dad used to read us stories every night before we went to bed. He was the person who tucked us in and who would get us up in the morning and drop us off at school. . . . He was the only stable thing that we knew in our lives."[75] In her extended statement to the Board of Pardons and Parole, Kayla further shares the length with which she has gone to reconcile with her mother:

71. Casey and Bennett, "Clemency Application," 44.

72. Casey and Bennett, "Clemency Application," 44–45.

73. See Zehr, "Restoring Justice," 21–33.

74. Casey and Bennett, "Clemency Application," 45.

75. "A Message from the Children of Kelly and Doug Gissendaner."

In February 1997, I lost my best friend and hero when I lost my dad, Douglas Morgan Gissendaner. He was my primary caregiver, and he always made sure that my brothers and I came first. . . . He made sure we knew what it meant to be unconditionally loved. The night my father was murdered the world was changed.

After my dad was killed, my brothers and I lived with Nanny, our maternal grandmother. When I was seventeen, I came home from school one day and saw that she had collapsed. I ran to her and discovered that she was dead. She had had a massive heart attack. My brothers and I lived separately from that point forward.

As I got older and was going through my teenage years, I stopped wanting to see my mother. I had visited her with Nanny when I was growing up, but when I got to college I decided to quit visiting her. . . . My mother continued to reach out to me but I ignored her. After about a year, I decided to meet with her again. . . . We had never talked about the crime or about what she had done. It was hard for both of us but she told me the terrible truth. As painful as that was, I realized then that I wanted to try to have a relationship with her again.

That was six years ago. Since that time, we have been able to have the mother/daughter relationship that had been missing for many years. My mom has changed so much over the past 18 years. We have such a wonderful relationship, and for the first time, I'm truly getting to know her.[76]

In the advocacy video, Kelly's son Dakota shares, too, about his long journey toward reconciliation: "I went through seven years of despising my mom, and me and my sister were talking one night, and she kept asking me, are you ever going to come back and see Mama?" In his clemency testimony, Dakota writes,

I told Kayla that I was just going to say what I needed to say and be done with my mom. Instead, I had the best visitation with her that I have ever had. And I can't believe it took me so long to realize that she is really my mom and I love her with all my heart no matter the situation. During the entire visit with my mom she told me that she loved me and asked what she could do for me. She apologized for all the hurt she had caused me and our family. She was a very different person than who I remembered or who I thought she was. During that visit my life changed for the better. I

76. "Statement of Kayla Gissendaner."

found my mother's unconditional love and a strong support I did not remember I had in my life.[77]

After reconnecting, Dakota began to visit Kelly regularly. "We wrote each other weekly. We laugh and cry together. We talk about my work and my classes at school. Mom holds my hand, strokes my hair, and assures me I can do anything or be anybody I want to be. She is my biggest cheerleader," he writes.[78]

In the testimony to the Board, Kayla concludes, "During the years since my dad's murder, I have struggled with the immense pain of losing him and the fact that my mother was involved in the murder. . . . I had to face what my mom had done and find a way to forgive her. . . . It was by no means an easy road, but I learned that forgiving my mother was the best way to truly honor my father."[79]

Together, Kelly and her children built from the ruins. They raised up the former devastation.

Hope Is Protest

In February 2015 the call came from Kelly's lawyers telling me that she had received her death warrant, including the precise date of the execution, which was set for two weeks later, Wednesday, February 25. Since the US Supreme Court had denied her last appeal in October 2014, Kelly had been living in a liminal space, fearing that each call or visit from her lawyers bore the bad news. A month before her last appeal was denied, she and I had set up fifteen-minute collect calls to add some structure to her week and to provide her with a small amount of extra support.

I had known for a while that because of my close relationship with Kelly I would speak at her clemency hearing, scheduled the day before the execution. We would be asking the Board of Pardons and Paroles to commute her sentence from death to life without parole. A year before, at the prompting of her dedicated team of lawyers, who guided her case for seventeen years through the appeals process, I wrote the letter to be submitted with her fifty-four-page application. It was filled, as we have seen, with

77. Casey and Bennett, "Clemency Application," 46.

78. Casey and Bennett, "Clemency Application," 46–47.

79. See "Message from the Children of Kelly and Doug Gissendaner." See also Casey and Bennett, "Clemency Application," 46. The statement about honoring their father was spoken multiple times by Kayla and Dakota.

testimonies not only from volunteers and friends incarcerated with her but also from officers, prison administrators, and even a former warden, most of whom had never written to the Board on behalf of someone in prison. When I got the February call, I quickly made arrangements for my courses and bought a plane ticket back to Atlanta for the following week, booked to arrive five days before the scheduled execution. That week marked the beginning of Lent, so, without much thought, I attended the Ash Wednesday service at the college chapel the day before I headed south.

Ash Wednesday is a time when Christians are called to confront and accept our mortality, as we ready ourselves for the forty days of Lent, a season of self-examination and renewal, a preparation itself for Easter and risen life. The ancient practice of making the sign of the cross with ashes reminds Christians that humanity belongs to God, from its beginning as dust of the earth to its end in the death and resurrection of Christ. The ashes are made from branches used on Palm Sunday the year before—(palms signifying those laid before Jesus as he entered Jerusalem, the city of his arrest, trial, and crucifixion.)

When the time came in the order of worship for the distribution of ashes, I made my way down the aisle toward my colleague Ramona Bouzard, who knew where I was traveling. She looked me in the eye and as she spread the oily ash across my forehead, she said in a slow and shaky voice, "Remember you are dust and to dust you will return." I accepted and fought those words, unsure how to make sense of them in that moment: What did it mean to affirm this word about mortality as I was preparing to fight the approaching execution?

The line, "remember you are dust," carries a peculiar comfort and power, so much so that people, regardless of whether or not they consider themselves religious, will line up on bustling city streets at lunch breaks to receive those words from a priest offering ashes as a public sacrament. This phenomenon, it seems to me, shows not so much that we are people who find comfort in our mortality (there's plenty of evidence that shows otherwise) but that we are a people yearning, at times, for permission to be limited and modest human beings. On a gut level, Ash Wednesday recalls and affirms our creatureliness.

The liturgical claim that we "are dust" comes from the creation narrative in Genesis 2, when God forms human beings "from the dust of the ground" and breathes into us the breath of life. Biblical scholar Ted Hiebert argues that the best translation of the Hebrew word is not "dust" but "soil," as in nutrient-rich topsoil.[80] If the image of dust connotes an insubstantial and fleeting state—something one can hardly hold in the palm of a hand, or if kicked up disappears into the air—the image of topsoil conveys the opposite. We are deeply connected to the earth, substantive, valuable, and loved as such. It is an important distinction. Still, whether understood as dust or soil, the Ash Wednesday proclamation tells us something central about who we are as human beings. We are not God, and we need not—nor should not—even try to be.

In his book *Creation and Fall*, a theological reading of Genesis 1 through 3, Bonhoeffer addresses the beauty of our God-given creaturehood and contrasts it with a desire to be like God. Central to the book's analysis is the theological significance of Adam and Eve eating from the prohibited tree of the knowledge of good and evil. The forbidden nature of the tree is rooted, for Bonhoeffer, in the "creatureliness" of human beings—a vocation characterized by limitation and freedom. Creaturely limits include obeying God's commands—do not eat from this particular tree—and creaturely freedom mirrors God's freedom, in which God chooses to be free not *from* others but *for others*. For Bonhoeffer, this is what it means to be created in the image of God; the *imago dei* refers to freedom. God's freedom for us is shown not only in the first act of creation but is the heart of the gospel proclamation.[81]

Creaturely limitation and freedom are inherently interconnected in our relationship with God and other human beings. In human relations, being free for others requires recognizing limits—our own limit and the limit of others. To recognize *my* limit is to honor the otherness of another person, to refuse to treat them as an extension of myself, to refuse to control them with my own will or demand. Recognizing limits also means respecting *the other person as a limit* I shall not violate. Instead of trying to master or control, we are to treat any person "as God's creature," Bonhoeffer writes, as the one "who stands beside me and constitutes a limit for me."[82]

For Bonhoeffer, the fall as depicted in Genesis 3 is a fall precisely from our creatureliness. When Adam and Eve eat from the tree of the knowledge of good and evil, they become "like god"—*sicut deus*—just as the serpent

---

80. Hiebert, "Retranslating Genesis 1–2." The Common English Bible translation, for which Hiebert was the lead translator of Genesis, translates Genesis 2:7: "the Lord God formed the human from the topsoil of the fertile land."

81. A longer version of this argument appears in McBride and Fabisiak, "Bonhoeffer's Critique of Morality."

82. Bonhoeffer, *Creation and Fall*, 99.

predicted (Gen 3:5). They now presume that the origin of the knowledge of good and evil resides in them and not in God, who forbade them from eating from that tree. Bonhoeffer's interpretation of the fall rests, then, on the juxtaposition of two ways of living before God: through the *imago dei* or by being *sicut deus*. While the image of God refers to humanity's creaturely freedom, limitation, and interdependence, trying to be "like god" entails breaking our limits as creatures by positioning ourselves as equal to God and superior to other human beings. It entails operating out of our own understanding of the knowledge of good and evil and setting ourselves up as judge, based on a moral paradigm we humans create. With this knowledge, humans assume we are equipped to judge the moral status of other human beings. We presume we are in a position to judge their moral worth, even the worthiness of their lives.

I have come to understand the significance of Ash Wednesday in this way, as a call to live as creatures made in the image of God, free only when we live for one another. The smudged ash reminds us of the limits that make that freedom possible and of the gift of our creaturehood. But the death penalty replicates the fall, in its erroneous attempt to be "like god," in its perverted sense of freedom, which falsely assumes we can find freedom for ourselves by being free *from* others. As the most extreme attempt at this false freedom, the death penalty does not reflect the Ash Wednesday truth that we "are but dust and to dust you will return." For that truth, rightly conceived, is not merely a description of our mortality (which is but one human limit); rather, it is a call to creaturehood and to a holy respect for every human limit. No, in its attempt to be free *from* others—to master and control—the death penalty is a power and principality that counters God's reign. Since our creatureliness makes each of us vulnerable to systemic and institutional powers strong enough to do us harm, we must advocate for the well-being of one another and proclaim the worthiness of each other's lives. Doing so reflects our fundamental interdependence as creatures made in the image of God. Being an advocate (the name the Bible gives the Holy Spirit) is a mark of the Spirit and a sure way to participate in the reign of God over against powers and principalities that condemn human beings (John 14:26).

Although I did not have this theological clarity at the time, nor the resources to sort out my emotions, I knew intuitively as I prepared to speak before the Board that I was entering a fundamentally untruthful situation, since clemency hearings are defined by a distorted sense of freedom.

Starting with the assumption that society should be free from Kelly, we were tasked with proving to a panel of men the worth of another human being, someone the prison system already classified as "condemned."[83]

As I flew to Atlanta, I assumed my primary role beyond the clemency hearing would be to accompany Kelly through visits in the days leading up to it. When I arrived, I learned that although I was on her "death watch" list and therefore able to visit her the day before and the day of the execution, I was not allowed to be added to her regular visitation list. I spent the weekend instead meeting with her lawyers and practicing my clemency speech alone in my room *ad nauseam*. As time drew closer, I realized that I was terrified of speaking before the Board, terrified not only of their authority but also of my inability to speak authentically into a situation that was inherently arbitrary and nonsensical. We knew that if the Board were to proceed with Kelly's execution, it would be the first time in the modern era of the death penalty, post-1976, that Georgia officials would be executing someone whom they knew was not the murderer. But this fact provided little comfort given the totalizing authority that the Board held.[84] I would be addressing five men who had the incomprehensible power to take or save Kelly's life and who need not show any guidelines or reasons for their opinions. The whole process had a wave of inevitability about it, interrupted only by moments of hope grounded in the reality of who Kelly had become.

My letter to the Board shared this reality, how I first met Kelly that morning in the classroom where she arrived beaming with excitement, and how six months later we continued to read theological texts, this time through the bars of her cell, including the sermon by Rowan Williams. I

---

83. At the time of Kelly's clemency hearing, the Parole Board members were Brian Owens, Albert Murray, Braxton Cotton, James Mills, and Terry Barnard. See https://pap.georgia.gov/past-members.

84. In 1972, in *Furman vs. Georgia*, the US Supreme Court held that the death penalty was being applied arbitrarily and therefore was unconstitutional under the eighth and fourteenth amendments. In 1976, in *Gregg vs. Georgia*, the Supreme Court ruled that Georgia's new capital punishment procedures were in keeping with the eighth amendment and executions resumed. As described in Kelly's second clemency application, the Georgia Board had granted clemency in the past to at least four co-defendants, like Kelly, who had not performed the murder (Casey and Bennett, "Emergency Application," 13–16). In Kelly's case, as we repeated in our media talking points, the person who physically committed Doug's murder, Gregory Owen, is serving a life sentence and could be eligible for parole by 2023. Owen admitted in post-conviction proceedings that he lied at trial about key facts that made Kelly look worse in the eyes of the jury.

told the men that comprised the so-called "mercy board" how Kelly had done and continued to do the incredibly difficult work of "going back to the memories of the painful, humiliating past and bringing them to redemption in the present . . . to Christ [who] comes to repair the devastation."[85] I joined the chorus of voices that had testified to how Kelly had gone back to her painful memories, increasingly took responsibility for them, and showed profound remorse. In my letter, I told the Board about our most recent visit on Christmas Day, how Kelly wanted me to know more fully her involvement in the crime, not just who she was now but who she was then. For most of the time that I knew her, Kelly could not speak directly about the crime because the case was pending, and her counsel wisely advised that she not talk about it in detail with anyone except the legal team. But once the appeals process was over, Kelly wanted me to know. I told the Board that the power of that moment, where she looked me in the eye and confessed concrete sins, where, in turn, I proclaimed to her the depth of God's forgiveness, will stay with me forever.

I told the Board that most poignant for Kelly were the writings of Jürgen Moltmann, known internationally as the theologian of hope, whom she read in my theology foundations course in prison. Kelly knew that I had a collegial friendship with Professor Moltmann and asked if it would be appropriate for her to write him. I said yes, certain he would write her back. Professor Moltmann was so impressed with Kelly and so moved by their correspondence that he asked me if I would bring him to meet her when he traveled from his home in Tübingen, Germany to Atlanta, Georgia, where he would be delivering the Reformation Day lecture at Emory University. This opportunity led to Professor Moltmann giving the keynote address at the theology graduation for Kelly's class in October 2011 and to a two-hour pastoral visit with Kelly and me. I told the Board that the time I shared with the two of them in that small visitation room will remain one of the most significant experiences of my life. In one sense, it would be hard to find two people more different in this world—a German academic who is one of the most widely read and respected theologians of the twentieth and twenty-first centuries and the only woman on Georgia's death row. Yet I was struck by how similar they were and how real the connection was between them on account of their journeys of faith.

Like Kelly, Professor Moltmann's conversion began in prison, when he was taken by the British as a prisoner of war in February 1945. Like Kelly,

---

85. Williams, *Ray of Darkness*, 65–66.

this was where his formal theological studies began. During this time, he, too, was dealing with a profound sense of loss, shame, and guilt while learning to navigate the ruins and cultivate hope.

Born in April 1926, Jürgen Moltmann's late childhood was marked by state youth movements like "the Hitler Youth, by confirmation classes, and a dancing class," all of which were meant "to contribute to our maturity," he writes in his autobiography, and for all of which he was "wholly unsuited."[86] His parents were not members of the National Socialist Party and did not support the Nazis but this, of course, did not stop him from being conscripted with the rest of his schoolmates into the air force auxiliaries in 1943. Between the winter of 1943 and 1945, Moltmann was drafted into the auxiliary, the antiaircraft unit, the labor service, and the German army. He was, as he says, "always shot at but never fired a shot myself, and that was all to the good."[87] Multiple times a friend was killed in battle next to him, at one point with a friend dying in his arms. From these moments on, he lived with "the guilt of survival" and "searched for the meaning of continued life."[88]

Moltmann's feelings of guilt were only intensified soon after these events when his father visited him and shared a horrendous discovery: "He had heard about the mass murder of Jews and had seen the mass graves himself." At risk to himself, "he wanted me to know as well. This completely put a stop to my willingness to serve," writes Moltmann. Knowing that the ongoing war was a "cover for crimes" such as this "embittered" him with a sense of his own "helplessness."[89] In February 1945, when he found himself "hungry and thirsty, filthy and covered with lice," surrounded by British and Canadian troops and alone in the German forest, he surrendered and was taken to a large camp in Belgium, which he describes as "frightful." Moltmann writes, "We had escaped the inferno, but now we were sitting behind barbed wire and had lost all hope." An "inward imprisonment of the soul" accompanied the POWs' "outward captivity," each of them trying to conceal their pain "behind an armour of untouchability and indifference." The conditions only got worse for the prisoners when the war ended in May 1945. "The end of the war . . . meant the end of the Nazi nightmare," he writes, "but the Red Cross declared that since there was no longer a

86. Moltmann, *Broad Place*, 13.
87. Moltmann, *Broad Place*, 22.
88. Moltmann, *Broad Place*, 17.
89. Moltmann, *Broad Place*, 20.

German state, they were no longer responsible for us."[90] The POWs continued to be held, but without regard for their basic material needs.

In August 1945, Moltmann was transferred to a prisoner of war camp on the coast of Scotland. There he had two experiences that healed his depression and gave him "new hope in life." The first was the hospitality of a few Scottish families, "who came to meet us, their former enemies" without reproach or blame. In the prison, the Scottish overseers showed the POWs pictures of the Belsen and Buchenwald concentration camps; through these images they were driven to see themselves through the eyes of the victims of the Nazi regime. Upon viewing them, "every patriotic feeling for Germany . . . collapsed and died," writes Moltmann. "Depression from the wartime destruction and captivity with no end in sight was compounded by a feeling of profound shame at having to share in shouldering the disgrace of one's own people"—a weight, he says, that has never left him. But from these Scottish families, the POWs "experienced a simple and warm common humanity which made it possible" for them to face what had happened "without repressing it and without growing callous." As a result of the Scottish families' hospitality and forgiveness, "we were able to laugh again," writes Moltmann.[91]

In the Scottish prison camp, he read the Bible for the first time. After an army chaplain distributed copies to the prisoners, Moltmann started reading the Bible each evening but without comprehending much until he came to the lament Psalms, especially Psalm 39:

> I am dumb and must eat up my suffering within myself.
> My life is nothing before thee.
> Here my prayer, O Lord, and give ear to my cry.
> Hold not though thy peace at my tears,
>   for I am a stranger with thee, and a sojourner, as all my fathers were.

"That was an echo from my own soul, and it called that soul to God," writes Moltmann. "I didn't experience any sudden illumination but I came back to these words every evening."[92] Soon after reading the Psalms, he read the entirety of the Gospel of Mark. When he came to the passion narrative and heard Jesus' cry from the cross, "My God, why have you forsaken me?," Moltmann felt stirring within him a conviction: "This is someone who

---

90. Moltmann, *Broad Place*, 25–27.

91. Moltmann, *Broad Place*, 28–29.

92. Moltmann, *Broad Place*, 30.

Edty H
J Moltma~

LIVED THEOLOGY ON DEATH ROW

understands you completely, who is with you in your cry to God and has felt the same forsakenness you are living now." He writes,

> I began to understand the assailed, forsaken Christ because I knew that he understood me. The divine brother in need, the companion on the way, who goes with you through this "valley of the shadow of death," the fellow-sufferer who carries you, with your suffering. I summoned up the courage to live again, and I was slowly but surely seized by a great hope for the resurrection into God's "wide space where there is no more cramping." This perception of Christ did not come all of the sudden or overnight, either, but it became more and more important for me.

He concludes, "Whenever I read the Bible again with the searching eyes of the God-forsaken prisoner I was, I am always assured of its divine truth."[93]

When, in the spring of 1946, he realized that he was going to remain in captivity longer than he anticipated, Moltmann applied to be sent to an educational camp, where younger prisoners could take the final examination that was required for university admission. He passed the English language test and was sent by train, with an armed guard, to Norton Camp in central England. The camp, established by the British YMCA and financed by a businessman from America, was divided into two schools, one that trained teachers and another that trained pastors for a post-war Germany. Moltmann attended lectures on both sides of the camp and in 1947 decided to become a pastor. His curriculum included all the required disciplines for ordination (Hebrew and Greek, Old and New Testament, systematic theology and ethics, and church history), with courses taught by both rising and established scholars, some of whom might be found on a syllabus today. They included both imprisoned professors and visiting ones who would voluntarily stay at the camp to teach for a set period of time in a kind of "enclosed monastic experience." The training program used books from the YMCA's prisoner aid program, like Bonhoeffer's 1937 text *Nachfolge* (later known in English as *The Cost of Discipleship*), the same copy of which Moltmann still has in his library today. "I have never again lived so intensive an intellectual life as I did in Norton Camp," Professor Moltmann writes.[94]

In the summer of 1947, while still a POW, Moltmann and other prisoners of war were invited to attend an international Christian conference. Wearing their wartime uniforms and bearing the shame of the Nazi

93. Moltmann, *Broad Place*, 30–31.
94. Moltmann, *Broad Place*, 32–33.

41

atrocities, they were welcomed "as brothers in Christ" by young Christians who had come from all over the world. A group of Dutch students asked to meet with the POWs in a formal setting, and in a kind of impromptu victim-offender dialogue, they told their stories "about the Gestapo terror in their country, about the killing of their Jewish friends, about the destruction of their homes" in raw detail. The Dutch Christians then spoke of Jesus as a bridge of reconciliation between them that could be crossed if the POWs "could confess the guilt of [their] people and ask for reconciliation." They did. Moltmann writes, "At the end we all embraced. For me that was an hour of liberation . . . and I returned to the camp with new courage."[95]

In his keynote address at the 2011 theology graduation in Georgia, Professor Moltmann spoke about the beginning of his theological vocation in prison, "When I first heard of your study of theology in prison, pictures of my youth and the beginning of my own theological studies emerged from the depth of my memory. Yes, I remember."

> My theological studies started in a poor prisoner-of-war camp after World War II. I was 18 years old when I became a Prisoner-of-War for more than 3 years. I was lucky: it was in Britain not in Siberia! In a camp of forced labor in Kilmarnock, Scotland, I read for the first time in my life the Bible and encountered Jesus. I had not decided for Christ, but I am certain Christ found me there when I was lost in sadness and desperation. He found me, as Christ has come to seek what is lost.
>
> I tried to understand what had happened to me. We had "a theology school behind barbed wire." . . . Excluded from time and the world, imprisoned professors taught imprisoned students. . . . We studied the Bible, church history and theology, but we also tried to come to terms with our death-experiences at the end of the war. Theology was for us at that time an existential experience of healing our wounded souls.
>
> These were the beginning of my theological studies and my first experiences of the Church of Christ: the Church in prison camps. Later I became a pastor and professor of theology, but deep in my heart, there is still sitting a frightened and sad POW.

Affirming the graduates' theological contributions to the "world-wide fellowship of all theologians," an "age old community" that includes "Augustine and Thomas Aquinas, Martin Luther and Dietrich Bonhoeffer," Moltmann continued,

95. Moltmann, *Broad Place*, 34.

Every Christian who believes and understands is a theologian, not only the professionals at Candler or Tübingen, every Christian! . . . You are really theologians and in fact excellent theologians. I have read a paper that Jenny McBride sent me, and I was impressed. My students at Tübingen could not have made it better. . . .

I would like to encourage you: Go on and take the next course in Theological Studies. And you must not only learn from other theologians, develop your own thoughts. We need your spiritual insight and theological reflections. . . . We need you: the theology in the world needs the theology in prison. . . . You are the Church! We are sisters and brothers in Christ Jesus.[96]

By the October 2011 graduation, Professor Moltmann and Kelly had exchanged a number of letters, ten in all, over a fifteen-month period. Their correspondence demonstrated not only that theology could be "an existential experience" of "healing wounded souls," but also, as he said in his first letter back to her, that "theology is a great passion and a journey of adventures and discoveries in the holy mystery of God."

Kelly had a unique passion for the academic discipline of theology, something rarely shared by the ordinary Christian, however devout. She had a unique interest in theology as a pattern of thinking and a seemingly natural ability to absorb its rhythms and make the ideas her own. I noticed this as she was reading my first book while I revised it, the way she would reflect on a theological truth in conversation with me that echoed an argument I had made, but that also was so thoroughly integrated into her own thinking that I never could have guessed from where she was drawing. In this way, she was the kind of student that every professor desires—continuing a legacy while forging a path of her own. This was the relationship she sought and found with Professor Moltmann—the opportunity not only to learn from him but also to try out her theological chops and play with new ideas.

The new ideas that Kelly played with, both in the certificate program and in her letters, connected the personal aspects of Christian faith with its social, public, and universal dimensions. In her graduation speech, Kelly summarized this dynamic:

As I studied the doctrines in biblical and theological courses, my task was to ask at every point what the doctrines had to say about my social as well as my devotional life, my everyday private and public worship, my life here and now as well as my life in the

96. Also published in McBride, *Radical Discipleship*, 200–201.

"world to come." Only when I asked these questions could I fulfill the task of a good theologian—one who speaks and thinks about both the true God and real human beings in the real world.

Like anyone rethinking her earlier theology and learning new frameworks, Kelly was in process. She embraced new ideas about the implications of Christian faith for social and political life, which were liberating to her, since they provided resources for her to further resist her death row condemnation. Yet she also needed time for these patterns of thinking to become secondhand, habitual. In her initial letter to Professor Moltmann, Kelly wrote about studying Christian hope in the theology foundations course, and she framed the topic through questions focused on the individual and personal aspects of faith: "(1) What is the Christian hope for individual persons? (2) What is going to happen to me and those whom I love?" Quoting the Apostles' Creed, she offered an answer, "I believe in the resurrection of the body and the life everlasting."

In his letter back to Kelly, Professor Moltmann answered her inquiry about individual persons first and did so "on a personal level," with a view toward what was animating her question, namely, a concern about what would happen to her at the moment of execution. Poignantly, he assured her that what Jesus says to the thief on the cross, he says to Kelly at her moment of death, "Today you will be with me in Paradise" (Luke 23:43). He writes, "Not in three days, not at the end of days. . . . This is the 'Today' of the eternal God, God's eternal presence." When Professor Moltmann addressed, in turn, her more explicitly personal question, he wrote in deeply pastoral language, "Kelly, God has embraced you already. . . . And the risen Jesus is waiting for you on the other side. You are expected."

In the same letter, Professor Moltmann pushed Kelly to see the personal aspects of faith as part of the universal promises of God and, in doing so, encouraged a deeper integration of the two. After describing the resurrection referred to in the Apostles' Creed as the "resurrection of life, not really of the 'dead,'" he writes, "The life we have lived from birth on in all the good and heavy moments will be raised, and when raised from death also healed from the wounds of life." He continues,

> But the hope for the coming of God and his new creation of all things is not only a personal one. Our personal hope is embedded in our universal hope, and our hope for the universe is: sin, lies and violence will disappear from the earth and peace and the righteousness of God will renew the earth. There is hope against

the terror in this world. We shall never give up anything or anyone, but pray for them. Resurrection means also: Death will be no
more, and the hell is broken, and the separation from God will
disappear when God is coming to dwell in his earth forever. What
we feel already now as the Indwelling of the Holy Spirit, will fill
the whole universe. The Spirit will be poured out on all flesh, and
this is not only Christian flesh, but all of humanity, and not only
human flesh, but all the living beings.

When Kelly responded in agreement—writing, "the resurrection happened
in this world. For Jesus himself and for us it means the renewal of human
life, not escape from it," and, "the loving and just rule of God was not just
something to be expected in the distant or even near future but something
that was happening before" the disciples' "very eyes"—Professor Moltmann
responded that her writing "deserves the best grades in a doctoral seminar."
He exclaimed in his letter, "You can teach! But apart from this quality, your
words are speaking to the heart. Try to tell it to others."

Kelly and Professor Moltmann continued this conversation over the
course of the next few letters, discussing the universal dimensions of hope,
namely, the relationship between the powers of evil and death and the cosmic work of Christ. Jesus, as Paul says, "disarmed" the powers and exposed
their violence when he died on the cross, making peace by delivering creation from them and reconciling "all things" on earth to himself (Col 1:20;
2:15). Kelly wrote, "The Crucified and Risen Christ who will come to overthrow all the powers of darkness and evil that spoil God's good creation
and human life in it has already triumphed over them and even now is at
work to complete the work he has begun." Moltmann agreed, emphasizing
the ethical relevance of Jesus' triumph and the Spirit's present work of making all things new: "The category 'new' is universal. This is not superfluous
speculation" but has "eminent ecological relevance" for how we value human life and care for creation. "Can I send you my book, 'The Coming of
God' (2000)?" he writes.

Kelly gladly welcomed the offer; in the meantime, she had been reading his autobiography, *A Broad Space*. She had read the section about his
book *Theology of Hope* five times already and shared that she now had "a
deeper hope than I ever thought I could have within these prison walls!"
Her understanding of the this-worldly nature of Christian hope was only
deepened as she read the section about his book on the Holy Spirit, *The
Source of Life*, a text in which Professor Moltmann explains "why reverence
for the life of all the living and why the spirituality of the body and the earth

had become so important to me." In *A Broad Space*, Moltmann writes, "My concern [in *The Source of Life*] was to turn the traditional spirituality of the soul, which in its love for God is oriented toward the world beyond," to what he argues is a more biblical understanding, "a spirituality of the senses, of the body, of the earth."[97] In *The Source of Life* he asks, "In the spirituality of the soul, men and women seek the other-worldly Spirit of the wholly other God. But what Spirit did the people experience in the biblical stories?" In the creation account, God's *ruach*—God's spirit—is breathed into the nostrils of the human being and becomes the breath of life itself. "So human beings sense the divine Spirit when they sense their own vitality with all their senses." In the Easter story, God's Spirit raises Jesus from the dead. In the Pentecost story, "God's Spirit is poured out on all flesh" (Acts 2:17). Moltmann observes, "the works of God always end in bodiliness" and "the kingdom of God comes '*on earth* as it is in heaven.'" All of this calls for a spirituality that deepens love for *this* life, "a spirituality of the wakened senses, a new mysticism of bodily life, and a new reverence for the earth."[98] And so, in his autobiography, in a passage that Kelly described as "the most beautiful words I have read in a very long time," Professor Moltmann creatively revises a famous passage from Augustine's *Confessions* to say:

> When I love God I love the beauty of bodies, the rhythm of movements, the shining of eyes, the embraces, the feelings, the scents, the sounds of all this protean creation. When I love you, my God, I want to embrace it all, for I love you with all of my senses in the creations of your love. . . .
>
> For a long time I looked for you within myself and crept into the shell of my soul, shielding myself with an armour of inapproachability. But you were outside—outside myself—and enticed me out of the narrowness of my heart into the broad place of love for life. So I came out of myself and found my soul in my senses, and my own self in others.
>
> The experience of God deepens the experiences of life. It does not reduce them. For it awakens the unconditional Yes to life. The more I love God, the more gladly I exist. The more immediately and wholly I exist, the more I sense the living God, the inexhaustible source of life and eternal livingness.[99]

97. Moltmann, *Broad Space*, 348.
98. Moltmann, *Broad Space*, 349.
99. Moltmann, *Broad Space*, 350.

Professor Moltmann's theology connects the love of God with an ever-deepening love for *this* life in *this* world, here and now: The more we love God, the more we love our own lives and respect the lives of others. Moltmann's theology of earthly love, which Kelly wholeheartedly embraced, echoes a passage from Bonhoeffer's *Letters and Papers from Prison*, where he writes, "It is only when one loves life and the earth so much that without them everything seems to be over that one may believe in the resurrection and a new world."[100] In one way or another, all of us who spoke at the clemency hearing on Tuesday, February 24—the day before the scheduled execution—were trying to convey how Kelly lived this theology through her love of God, others, and herself.

Aware that my words were imperfect and incomplete, I practiced my five-minute speech for the clemency hearing one last time early Tuesday morning. I headed downtown and shuffled my way into a small court room filled with people advocating on Kelly's behalf, a community of people, most of whom I knew: pastors, chaplains, theology instructors, a formerly incarcerated woman, and Kelly's children, also victims of the crime, who begged these five men to spare their mother's life. For over four hours, together, we documented the fruits of her redemption: reconciliation with her college-aged children, ministry to incarcerated women full of despair whom no one else could reach, counsel to troubled youth who visit the prison, and daily concern for others. As I sat in the back row waiting my turn, I listened to the truth of her life be boldly proclaimed. The air was thick with the presence of God in this truth-filled speech.

The air was also thick with a cloud of suspicion demonstrated, no less, through the theological assertions made by the Board of Pardons and Paroles. Kelly's lawyers had advised our community of religious advocates that although it was appropriate to tell Kelly's story in the language of her transformation—the particular language of Christian faith—we should do so without making sweeping theological proclamations or engaging in theological debate, a request with which we all heartily agreed. We were not there to preach, nor were we advocating that Kelly should be given mercy because she was a Christian. Rather, we were arguing that she was a restored human being who had an enormous amount to give if granted life in prison. In a startling dismissal of church-state separation, though, the Board of Pardons and Paroles, all self-identified Christians, initiated a series of theological questions, interrogations that revealed what theologian

---

100. Bonhoeffer, *Letters and Papers* (Touchstone ed.), 157.

Walter Wink calls "the myth of redemptive violence."[101] "What about the thief on the cross? Jesus could have used his power to get him down, but he didn't," one member said with conviction. "Doesn't the fact that Jesus died on the cross show that good can come from death?" asked another in earnest. Later in a prayer vigil for Kelly, Reverend Yolanda Thompson responded to these questions with appropriate indignation. She said, "We were asked, 'Why would Jesus not stop his own execution on the cross?' Really? In the Bible Belt in Georgia, you're asking a room filled with pastoral leaders *that* question? Really? Why did Jesus die on the cross? *Why?* So that Kelly can *live* . . . and 'declare the works of the Lord.'"[102]

After the Tuesday morning hearing, holding in tension apprehension and hope, I raced to the prison to see Kelly before visitation ended, the first opportunity I had to see her since Christmas Day. There, she and a few companions were anxiously awaiting news of the hearing. "Your children were amazing," I said as others arrived, and together with nervous excitement we shared the details of every testimony we could recall.

Early Wednesday morning I made my way back to the prison under a winter advisory warning, unsure what the day would hold. By the time I arrived, the execution scheduled for that night had been postponed to five days later because of the possibility of snow, but we still awaited the Board's decision. To pass the time, our small group of visitors played "I Spy" with Kelly in a small and completely bare visitation cell, fully aware of the absurdity of the game and our attempt to distract ourselves from the pending news. To stay hopeful, we playfully imagined what it would be like for Kelly once she was living in "general population," sharing visitation space with the rest of the incarcerated women the next room over. We joked about the crowds of visitors swarming the vending machines, her pushing up against the rope like everyone else, calling out over the commotion, "They're out of burgers? Okay, get me the pizza instead!" Then the call came that stopped us in our tracks.

Kelly was ushered into the next room to take the call from her lawyers. The five of us in the visitation room grabbed each other's hands, stared stoically at the wall, and took deep breaths as we waited to hear if this woman full of life and purpose would be executed by the state in just a few days. Minutes later, Kelly walked past the window of the visitation cell and turned the corner shaking her head. "We lost, we lost," she said underneath

101. Wink, *Engaging the Powers*, 13–32.
102. "Vigil of Light, Life, and Solidarity for Kelly."

a stream of tears. Her daughter slammed her fist on the table and fell into a heap on the floor. Hours later, reflecting on the horror, Kelly would say to me, "I had to pick my baby up off the ground." Leaving her alone with her children, we huddled together in the hallway, and holding on to one another, we wept.

In the weeks before the clemency hearing I reflected on how my mind and body might process this all, wondering if I would be able to wrap my head around the surreal nature of it enough to feel any emotion at all. As one who had struggled with depression, I had known inner darkness, a dark night of the soul that at its worst feels like an abyss, an interior hold that seems as though it may never be lifted. Until that moment, though, I had never experienced this abyss outside of myself—the finality of what transpired, the knowledge that no amount of trying can budge this external reality, where there is no turning back, where there is no person to whom you may direct your complaint, where nothing can stop what is now, in all absolute terms, inevitable. This is the power of death. This is what it means to be surrounded by what Paul calls the powers and principalities of death. As others rotated back into the room with Kelly, I sat in the vast, empty visitation hall weeping into this void. Our last hours of visitation were spent mostly in shared silence as we all continued to absorb the news together, a silence broken only by sporadic words addressed to Kelly: "Your life is so valuable. We love you so much."

Until, at the end of visitation, two members of Kelly's legal team burst in, breaking through the silence. Her investigator marched straight up to her, stopped Kelly's attempt at a consoling hug, and instead grabbed her face, pulled her close, and said, "Listen, we are not giving up. Remember Daniel in the lion's den? You are in the lion's den, my friend, but this is not over." Her fervor startled me out of despair, and I breathed in new life.

I do not know when it exactly happened, perhaps sometime in the hour and a half drive back from the prison, but a renewed resolve welled up within me, a determination that Kelly's execution would not happen in silence, behind closed doors, without the world watching. I did not necessarily think her life could be saved, except by her lawyers who were working around the clock, but I did think her story could be told. We could raise her voice, demanding that her life be witnessed and this execution be condemned. When I got back to my brother's home in Atlanta, without much of a plan I reached out to a colleague at *The New York Times*, simply wondering if the theology certificate and the story of Professor Moltmann's friendship might be of interest for his weekly religion piece. As I did so, I noticed Facebook and cell phone messages from a few close friends. A group of about twenty, all of whom were connected in various ways to the prison theology program, were already gathering to strategize next steps: seminary faculty, theology certificate instructors, pastors and priests, doctoral students and seminarians, and a formerly incarcerated woman who credited Kelly with her own transformation. That night in the living room of a dear friend the #KellyOnMyMind campaign was born. Bolstered by the embodied hope of her lawyers and these companions, I wrote on social media that night: "Our message is the beauty and concrete value of Kelly's life. . . . We still cling to a sliver of hope."

In that living room we met every night to strategize under the organic leadership of pastor-activists and scholar-activists who, although not professional organizers, drew on previous activism and knowledge of social change. Within a day or two, *The New York Times* piece was out, getting picked up by other media outlets from CNN and *The Washington Post* to Fox News and the Christian Broadcasting Network.[103] Kelly's story was impacting Christians across the political divide, pushing the logic of Christian faith to its outermost limits, pressing Christians to reexamine and reaffirm the truths we proclaim about repentance, forgiveness, redemption, and hope. In the five short days leading up to the rescheduled execution, we launched a major social media campaign reaching over four million people, wrote for *Huffington Post* and CNN.com, gathered letters from religion scholars around the world who advocated for Kelly as their theological colleague, started Faith Leader and Groundswell petitions and delivered over 80,000 signatures to the governor's office. We mapped out talking points, made targeted phone calls, published press releases, held a press conference and an action at the state capitol, produced short documentaries, hosted a prayer vigil, and sparked vigils in seminaries across the country. And we responded to numerous local, national, and international interview requests. The movement was happening so quickly we could barely keep up. Each strategic decision bore enormous weight and one risky decision about messaging, timing, or placement led to another. Casting aside our day jobs as much as we could, we threw ourselves into the work, every concrete act, in Moltmann's words, arousing "passion for the possible" and throwing open

---

103. See Oppenheimer, "Death Row Inmate Finds Common Ground"; McBride, "Georgia Death Row Inmate Finds Path Back to Hope"; Aaron, "Case for Clemency?"; and a partial list of other articles at http://www.kellyonmymind.com/articles/.

the future.[104] This was our participation in God's liberating power, already revealing itself in threats of snow. This was our Spirit-filled resistance to evil and death.

We told Kelly's story everywhere and every way we could, most poignantly in a series of short documentaries, one of which quite literally raised her voice. "Because Kelly is behind bars she cannot speak to you herself," the documentary begins, "so we ask you to listen to the words she has written as we lend our voices to lift her story." Drawing on the art of spoken word, a number of diverse voices read lines from her clemency confession and graduation speech:

> It is impossible to put into words the overwhelming sorrow and remorse I feel for my involvement in the murder of my husband, Douglas Gissendaner. / There is just no way to capture the depth of my sorrow and regret. I would change everything if I could. / I will never understand how I let myself fall into such evil but I have learned firsthand that no one, not even me, is beyond redemption through God's grace and mercy. /
>
> Hope is still alive. Despite a gate or guillotine hovering over my head, I still possess the ability to prove that I am human. / Labels on anyone can be notoriously misleading and unforgiving things, / but no matter the label attached to me, I have the capacity and unstoppable desire to accomplish something positive and to have a lasting impact. / Even prison cannot erase my hope and conviction that the future is not settled for me, or anyone. / I have placed my hope in the God I now know. / I rely on the steadfast and never ending love of God.

Driven by resurrection hope, we ended the documentary with these words: "As long as Kelly has breath, hope is still alive. So, we must act while there is still time. Tell Governor Deal he DOES have the power to halt this execution. Tell Georgia's Board of Pardons and Paroles that there is STILL TIME to reverse their decision."[105]

One of the most encouraging parts of the campaign, for me, was the outpouring of letters sent to Governor Nathan Deal and the Parole Board by religion scholars and religious leaders from North America and even Europe, who drew on their own theological traditions and expertise to advocate for Kelly as a theological colleague.[106] Most of the letters came

104. Moltmann, *Theology of Hope*, 35.

105. See "Kelly Gissendaner."

106. As part of our campaign, we offered a template that scholars could use as they

from prominent scholars in the fields of dogmatic, pastoral, or political theology, biblical studies, or Christian ethics; leaders in theological education like presidents and deans of seminaries; and presiding bishops from multiple denominations. Together, their brief words offered a rich tapestry of biblical, theological, and ethical wisdom that spoke both to the meaning of Kelly's transformation and to the injustice of the death penalty itself. Sounding like one of Paul's own epistles, one scholar (the author of the systematic theology textbook we used in the theology foundations course) opened his letter this way: "As a retired professor of theology who spent close to fifty years in theological education and in the service of the Gospel of Jesus Christ, I urge you to commute the execution of Kelly Gissendaner," while another wrote "as part of the international community of theologians . . . to express solidarity" with Kelly.[107]

Many of the letters appealed to Kelly's transformation and "the central conviction of the Christian tradition that redeemed sinners are meant by God to live out their redemption as a witness to the power of God's love."[108] As one systematic theologian wrote, "When Christians confess their sin they petition the Lord for forgiveness as well as for 'time for the amendment of life.' The execution of Ms. Gissendaner on Monday would cut her off from any such time for further amendment of life, the signs of which are already clear and the great benefits" of her life for others "are attested by her past Warden and other Correctional staff."[109] A pastoral theologian wrote, "Please spare her life, for her sake but also for our collective sakes as citizens" who need models that make evident "the possibility" of human transformation.[110] Likewise, a religious ethicist wrote, "If the life even of a convicted murderer can be turned around and so radically redirected, then none of us is without hope."[111]

Some letters emphasized the hard work of living as a forgiven human being—of "working out one's salvation" as Paul says in his letter to the Philippians (2:12)—especially in light of the magnitude of the crime:

---

crafted their letters. We also asked that letters emailed to Governor Deal and the Board be copied to me. I received close to 200 letters.

107. Migliore, unpublished letter, in the author's possession, 2015. Muers, unpublished letter, in the author's possession, 2015.

108. Winn, unpublished letter, in the author's possession, 2015.

109. Ziegler, unpublished letter, in the author's possession, 2015.

110. Dykstra, unpublished letter, in the author's possession, 2015.

111. Amesbury, unpublished letter, in the author's possession, 2015.

"The meaning of Kelly's crime can never be erased. Even her death cannot change what has been done. . . . Please allow her the opportunity to live out her redemption, which is in reality the more difficult burden we have all been called to bear." And in that same letter, "To put an end to [Kelly's life] in the name of justice would in fact be to cede too much power to evil, and to place too little faith in the possibility of good's eventual triumph. . . . As a society we can do better than to compound death in search of an imagined final balancing of the scales. Death should here be denied the last word."[112]

Other letters appealed to the relationship between God's mercy and justice, in which mercy and justice "kiss," as Psalm 85 states: "I implore you to bring mercy and justice together and decide in favor of clemency," wrote one scholar.[113] "In the Christian tradition, the God of justice and the God of mercy are not two gods but one. The loving and redeeming mercy of God . . . serves justice by transforming and healing lives," wrote a doctoral student.[114] "We implore you not just to show mercy, but, more basically, to enact a more appropriate justice," echoed a letter from a seminary dean.[115] Likewise, appealing to the biblical truth that God's justice is fundamentally restorative, not retributive, a Reformed theologian wrote, "All who follow the way of Jesus believe in forgiveness and transformation by the grace of God, not in retaliation as the definitive and necessary form of justice for a wrong committed."[116] Naming how easily the call for retributive justice masks a human desire for vengeance, a Quaker theologian wrote, "In this situation, demanding her death constitutes not an act of justice, but an act of vengeance that stands in contradiction to the basic tenets of Christian faith as well as to the principles of human dignity and human rights."[117] Or as three bishops in the Evangelical Lutheran Church of America wrote, "In the end, we cannot, as Christian leaders, accept revenge as a justification for state sponsored execution. . . . We pray for you in this difficult time. And we pray that you will choose life."[118]

Some of the letters addressing God's justice explicitly stated concern for the victim's family (Doug's extended family who supported the

112. Amesbury, unpublished letter, in the author's possession, 2015.

113. Cheng, unpublished letter, in the author's possession, 2015.

114. Wilton, unpublished letter, in the author's possession, 2015.

115. Bader-Saye, unpublished letter, in the author's possession, 2015.

116. Migliore, unpublished letter, in the author's possession, 2015.

117. Muers, unpublished letter, in the author's possession, 2015.

118. Eaton et al., unpublished letter, in the author's possession, 2015.

execution), alongside advocacy for Kelly and her children. One chaplain in a Virginia women's prison wrote, "I will not pretend to understand what the victim's family has gone through over these long years. . . . Retribution is a normal and natural response to trauma. . . . The victim's family . . . needs support, opportunities to share their stories and resources for healing from trauma. The execution will not address these ongoing needs."[119] A Christian ethicist offered a complementary witness that concern for victim's rights can and should move beyond the call for death. "I send this letter as one whose family was victimized by violent murder," he wrote. "My grandfather was killed by a man who was tried and convicted. I carry a profound experience of yearning for justice and yet at no point have I ever wished for a death sentence for my family's perpetrator. A nation that kills its citizens is a nation that holds no value for human life."[120] Other letters shared concern for the children as victims, who made clear that they wanted Kelly to live. "As a mother," some wrote, or "as a parent, I ask you to consider the devastating pain and grief of her children."[121]

The issue, it seems to me, wasn't that the five Christians comprising the Parole Board thought that God would not forgive Kelly or show her mercy in heaven. Rather, it was that their other-worldly theology assumed God's forgiveness and mercy had little or nothing to do with our lives here on earth. (I confess, I cannot help but think that it was their belief that Kelly *would* "go to heaven" that eased their consciences in an increasingly high-profile case.) These professed Christians could also divorce justice from mercy because they served as representatives of a criminal legal system that characteristically shows material concern only for victims who support the state's intent to carry out the full extent of the law, in this case Doug's extended family, not their children. In fact, Kelly's children were never contacted or assisted by anyone in a state or county office for victim's rights. In light of the carceral system's clear preference for retribution over restoration, one letter powerfully admonished the Board to connect their theology to public ethics: "God has shown mercy to Ms. Gissendaner already. I beg you and I implore you: Do likewise!"[122]

Some scholars appealed to authoritative thinkers within the Christian tradition who wrote about the necessary link between theology and public

---

119. Powell, unpublished letter, in the author's possession, 2015.

120. Conley, unpublished letter, in the author's possession, 2015.

121. Amesbury, unpublished letter, in the author's possession, 2015.

122. Lösel, unpublished letter, in the author's possession, 2015.

life, like the fourth-century bishop Augustine of Hippo, arguably the single most influential Christian theologian for Protestants and Catholics alike. Two letters drew on Augustine's own witness as a bishop who advocated for people under sentences of death. One cites a letter in which this church father "makes an especially strong appeal on behalf of those who have confessed their sins and sought to reform their lives, as Ms. Gissendaner has done."[123] Another writes about Augustine's concern that life be respected: "'Take action against the crime,'" not against the bodily health of the person, Augustine implores one judge, "'in order to liberate the human being.'"[124]

Catholic moral theologian Tobias Winright, also a former corrections officer and reserve police officer, published an open letter to the Board, urging them to uphold an ethic of life. In the letter, Winright draws on Catholic social teaching and the writing of recent popes. He shares how fifteen years earlier, when visiting St. Louis, Pope John Paul II asked the then-Governor of Missouri to commute the death sentence of Darrell Mease, "and the governor complied with his request." The Pope also used that moment to call for the abolition of the death penalty. John Paul wrote,

> The new evangelization calls for followers of Christ who are unconditionally pro-life: who will proclaim, celebrate, and serve the Gospel of Life in every situation. A sign of hope is the increasing recognition that the dignity of human life must never be taken away, even in the case of someone who has done great evil. . . . I renew the appeal . . . for a consensus to end the death penalty, which is both cruel and unnecessary.

Winright's letter continues, "Current Catholic teaching views executions carried out by the state authorities as morally justified if it is 'the only possible way of effectively defending the lives against an unjust aggressor.' . . . Paragraph 2267 of the Catechism of the Catholic Church adds, 'Today . . . the cases in which the execution of the offender is an absolute necessity are "very rare, if not practically nonexistent."'"[125]

Echoing the admonition that followers of Jesus must "serve the Gospel of Life in every situation," other letters argued that a pro-life stance requires nonviolent alternatives to address harm. "The world will not be a better place if this child of God is executed. Rather, we will have returned violence for violence, and we will all be diminished," wrote one seminary

---

123. Lamb, unpublished letter, in the author's possession, 2015.

124. Lösel, unpublished letter, in the author's possession, 2015.

125. Winright, "Open Letter to Gov. Nathan Deal."

president.[126] A longtime death penalty abolitionist and Catholic moral theologian was even more explicit. A respect for life demands that we reject "the lie" that "more violence makes us safer."[127] The violence inherent to it only brings guilt on all "who conduct a sentence of death," wrote another scholar, and causes further harm to a wide range of people in its reach.[128] As the chaplain at the Virginia women's prison witnessed during the execution of Teresa Lewis in 2010, "When counseling with staff and [residents of the prison] during the execution I was astonished by the depth of emotion and anguish connected with this woman's death."[129]

Perhaps the greatest challenge when addressing the Board was the popularly held belief that the Bible supports the death penalty. This was dramatically shown during a clemency hearing a friend witnessed, when one Board member explicitly stated, as he patted his Bible, that he was able to do his job "because of this." If the late evangelical ethicist Glen Stassen were still living, he would have surely written a letter rehearsing the argument he made in an essay written for Christian jurors who tended to believe the same thing. In his essay, "Biblical Teaching on Capital Punishment," Stassen examines explicit scriptural references to the death penalty and argues that there is a "seeming contradiction" found in the Old Testament Torah and the Mishnah, the oral interpretation of the Torah written between 200 BCE and 200 CE. The contradiction is this: While the death penalty is prescribed for a long list of crimes and transgressions, it is either unenforced or made virtually impossible to enforce. Through this seeming contradiction, Stassen argues that the Torah is affirming two moral principles: "the profound moral seriousness about obeying God's will" and the profound moral "seriousness about the sacredness of human life."[130]

In his essay, Stassen also examines the many biblical characters who had once committed murder or other acts that fell under the death penalty but were used instead as protagonists in God's salvation narrative, like Moses or David. And he shows that every time the death penalty is mentioned in the New Testament, it is "clearly presented as an injustice," be it the beheading of John the Baptist, the crucifixion of Jesus by the Roman Empire,

---

126. Olson, unpublished letter, in the author's possession, 2015.

127. Gathje, unpublished letter, in the author's possession, 2015.

128. Berlis, unpublished letter, in the author's possession, 2015.

129. Powell, unpublished letter, in the author's possession, 2015.

130. Stassen, "Biblical Teachings," 121–22.

or the stoning of Stephen and other followers of Jesus' way.[131] Some of the letters to the governor and Board highlighted these biblical passages, like when Jesus says to the crowd surrounding the woman caught in adultery, "Let anyone among you who is without sin be the first to throw a stone at her" and to the woman herself, "Has no one condemned you? . . . Neither do I condemn you" (John 8:7–8).[132] Or, as one seminarian said, "I write to you as one who draws on the inspiration of Christianity's greatest theologian, the Apostle Paul of Tarsus, who openly played a role in the murder of followers of Jesus (Acts 7:54–8:1) before his own conversion. What would be of our faith—of our world—if the mercy of God had not been great enough to allow this murderer to live?"[133]

Finally, Stassen's essay on biblical teachings emphasizes a central theme spanning the Old and New Testaments, namely, justice for the poor and oppressed. While the Roman Empire in Jesus' day reserved crucifixion for slaves and political dissidents, the United States reserves the death penalty for an analogous group—those who are poor or working class, like Kelly, and cannot afford adequate legal counsel during their trials. Within that group, the US reserves the death penalty disproportionately for minoritized racial groups, especially those who are Black. And while the death penalty's racial bias may not at first seem to apply to Kelly's case, it is relevant in the aggregate. It is the Southern, former slave-holding states—the states that maintained white supremacy after emancipation through racial terror like lynching—that have the most active execution chambers to this day.[134] We may understand the death penalty, then, as a racist structure that traps people of color as well as poor whites in its grip. As Episcopal Bishop of Atlanta Robert Wright wrote in an open letter, "Governor Deal, capital punishment is simply bloodlust. It is state-sanctioned mob violence and lynching, political expediency and tough-on-crime posturing. Capital punishment does not deter crime. Most importantly, you know it is not the will of God as revealed to us in the life and teachings of Jesus of Nazareth."[135]

131. Stassen, "Biblical Teachings," 125.

132. Lösel, unpublished letter, in the author's possession, 2015.

133. Ogi, unpublished letter, in the author's possession, 2015.

134. See Equal Justice Initiative, https://eji.org/issues/death-penalty/.

135. Wright, "An Open Letter to Governor Nathan Deal." Bishop Wright served as a primary spokesperson at a press conference for Kelly in March 2015; this open letter was written in response to a death penalty case in 2014. On Jesus' teachings, see Stassen, "Biblical Teachings," 121–26. In the Sermon on the Mount, Jesus says, "You have heard it said 'an eye for an eye' . . . But I say to you, 'do not set yourself in violent or revengeful

While many of the letters focused on Kelly's transformation, scholars and religious leaders also made vital points about the grave injustices of the death penalty, like its targeted demographic, that should inspire advocacy for anyone on death row, regardless of their degree or lack of change. "According to Christian faith every human being is a creature and image of God independent of a person's behavior," writes one scholar.[136] Appealing to the inherent dignity of every human being, professors and students from Carleton College in Minnesota sent dozens of letters from multi-faith perspectives making the same claim: "Christian, Jew, Buddhist, Muslim, Jain, Sikh, atheist—whatever our personal conviction, many of us have been following Kelly's story and have been horrified at the thought of her execution," wrote a Carleton anthropology professor.[137] Similarly, a Georgia State professor wrote, "Colleagues in theological studies are writing emails like this that ask that you consider the Christian faith's tradition. . . . My reasons for writing do not derive from a theological position. Instead, I urge you to commute Ms. Gissendaner's execution because I hope to raise my daughter in a state and nation that sees value in every human life and that does not practice retributive justice. I write in solidarity with Ms. Gissendaner, who despite her failings, is a person deserving of life."[138]

Although our campaign urged advocates to address letters to Governor Deal and the Board of Pardons and Paroles, in truth, there was no obvious place to direct our complaint. The Georgia legislator had passed a law removing the governor's power to commute sentences from death to life a few years earlier, and the Board had already made their decision. Indeed, the governor's public response to the flood of messages he received was to appeal to his *lack* of authority and wash his hands. We sought to expose his Pilate-like response and flood his office nonetheless—reminding

---

resistance to an evildoer." The Old Testament rule of retaliation, "an eye for an eye," was meant to limit vengeance, not require it. In the Gospels Jesus places even greater limits on the desire for revenge: "But I say . . . do not return evil for evil. . . . But I say to you . . . love your enemies" (Matt 5:17–43).

136. Faber, unpublished letter, in the author's possession, 2015.

137. Feldman-Savelsberg, unpublished letter, in the author's possession, 2015. Another example of multi-faith solidarity was a Tibetan Buddhist Puja (ceremony) for Kelly offered by the monks of Drepung Loseling Monastery in Atlanta. During the theology program, Kelly took a course on Cognitively-Based Compassion Training taught by Loseling community member Brendan Ozawa-de Silva. In February 2015, members of the Loseling community requested prayers for Kelly from 3,000 monks at the main monastery in India.

138. Basset, unpublished letter, in the author's possession, 2015.

him that he did have political influence over the Board since he appointed its members.

At an evening vigil the Sunday before the scheduled execution, I read Luke 18, particularly relevant since the governor had released a statement earlier that week telling people to "quit bothering" him about Kelly. The passage from Luke reads,

> Then Jesus told them a parable about their need to pray always and not lose heart. He said, "In a certain city there was a judge who neither feared God nor had respect for people. In that city there was a widow who kept coming to him and saying, 'Grant me justice against my opponent.' For a while he refused; but later he said to himself, 'Though I have no fear of God and no respect for anyone, yet because this widow keeps bothering me, I will grant her justice, so that she may not wear me out by her continual coming.'"

"We have come here tonight to bother Governor Nathan Deal," I said to a packed chapel. "We have come here to wear out the Board of Pardons and Paroles with our cry for justice—restorative, merciful justice. We have come here tonight because we are not giving up."

Earlier that Sunday morning, I visited with Kelly one last time, rotating in and out of the visitation room with family and close friends, since she planned to spend Monday's short morning visitation alone with her children. Kelly lived the best she could in the present moment, soaking in the time together—laughter led seamlessly into tears and back again. I watched as she and her stepmother, her last living parent, said goodbye: grasping hands, wailing, and pleading with one another to remember how much they are loved. Later I went to make a phone call to ask my ride to pick me up a little bit later, since visitation lasted longer than I had thought. An officer had given me permission to use a phone at the prison entrance, but I unknowingly crossed an invisible line that ended my visitation, and I was not permitted to go back. "I didn't even say goodbye," I said in a state of shock to an unyielding officer. That night, as I drove to the prayer vigil, Kelly called. I pulled off I-75 into a hotel parking lot and spoke to her for the fifteen minutes the collect call allowed. "Kelly, this doesn't feel real; I don't know how to say goodbye. We are still fighting for you," I said, as I tried to share all the beautiful things being spoken and written about her. "I feel everyone's love," she said, "I do." With just a few seconds left on the call I stammered, "The only thing I feel confident of is that Jesus will be there with you tomorrow night. I know he will be." "I know he will be, too," Kelly said, as our phone call ended.

On Monday evening, a group of us traveled to Jackson, Georgia, to the site of the men's prison that houses the death chamber. Some of our group headed to the grounds where a few hundred people would keep vigil, including a handful of women who had been in prison with Kelly. A few of us went on to New Hope House, a ministry that provides hospitality to families who visit men on death row as well as a base on execution nights for loved ones and lawyers, a sanctuary tucked away from the media and crowds where they can receive as much information as the lawyers in contact with the Attorney General's office can provide. The execution was scheduled for 7 PM, but as often happens there were several delays as we waited for the Supreme Court to rule on appeals to the higher courts. Hours later those last-minute appeals were denied.

More hours passed and finally we heard that there might be a complication with the lethal injection. Information was spotty, until finally, close to 11 PM, the Department of Corrections issued a last-minute postponement due to an unidentified problem with the compounded drug. It appeared to be "cloudy."[139] All planned executions in Georgia were temporarily postponed and would resume once the analysis of the drugs was complete.

Cheers rang out at the vigil on prison grounds. At New Hope House, we breathed a collective sigh of relief as we took in the news. Inside the women's prison in B Unit, a number of women had gathered around the television praying until the coverage seemed to end. They dispersed under the assumption that the execution had taken place until a woman who had been listening to the radio burst down the hall shouting, "She's alive! She's alive!"

Waiting in the holding cell next to the gurney, having no idea what was going on, Kelly also heard through the local news that there was "more drama in the Gissendaner case."

The next morning, headlines read, "Religious leaders see delay as an act of God." Tweets proclaim: "Snow. Cloudy Drugs. @GovernorDeal @GAParoleBoard @SCOTUSblog call this off before the plagues and swarms of locust arrive!" And editorials asked, "What else must God do?"[140]

---

139. See "News Coverage on Kelly's Case."

140. Kuruvilla, "Religious Leaders See Delay as an Act of God," *Huffington Post.* Cook, "The Butterfly in the Death Chamber," *Chattanooga Times.*

Months later, as we awaited another death warrant, Kelly's investigator told me, "The more I've thought about it the more convinced I've become that Kelly's life was saved that night because of the work you all did to make sure the world was watching. The Department of Corrections didn't have to stop that execution on account of the drugs."

On Good Friday, as I walked across the prison compound with Malaika, a student in the theology program, she told me that the delay of Kelly's execution reawakened her faith and gave her back her strength. "It had been so long since I had seen God move," she said. Still reeling from the experience just a few weeks before, I asked—more for me than for her—"What if the worst still happens? How will that affect your faith?" "I've thought about that a lot," Malaika responded. "All I can say is that I needed to know that God is still moving. Now I know."

We lived in this knowledge of God's movement for seven months and in the tension inherent in it—the tension between God's work and human agency, that liminal space where hope dwells.

Kelly's and my fifteen-minute collect calls resumed when she was able to use a phone a few weeks later. She told me how militarized COBRA officers burst into the visitation room moments after she had said her final goodbye to her children, and rushed at her shouting, "Against the wall! Get up against the wall!" as her children, still looking on, exited the room. She told me how she was driven back to her cell that night after the stayed execution, only to awaken to orders to pack her belongings once again. As the van passed Jackson Prison a few hours into the trip, she breathed a sigh of relief, assuming rightly that she was not heading back to the execution chamber but to Pulaski Prison for Women instead. There, in unfamiliar environs, removed from her former prison community, and more than three hours from her family, she would stay until her next execution date.

In early June Kelly told me that I could get on her official visitation list for the summer and see her on the weekends. For three Sundays I drove down county roads, deep into the rural South, past cotton fields and Confederate flags, and I thought of the connection between slavery and prisons in this Christ-haunted South. Lee Griffith writes that during the experience of exile, Israel learned the connection between enslavement and imprisonment. Their lesson was this: "The God who frees the slave frees the prisoner too." Griffith writes, "The biblical word regarding prisoners is both simple and scandalous: liberty for the captives. . . . The Bible identifies the prison with the spirit and power of death. . . . Whenever we cage people"—and, we may of course add, whenever we execute them—"we are in reality fueling and participating in the same spirit [Christians] claim to denounce."[141] As I drove through this plantation land, now the soil upon which the prison industrial complex grows, I thought of Frederick Douglass's words, "Between the Christianity of this land, and the Christianity of Christ, I recognize the widest possible difference." And I heard echoes of the pained question of Dr. King: "Who is their God?"[142]

The summer visits were hard. Kelly was in a state of depression I had never seen her in and the weight of uncertainty was wearing on me, too. In theory, she was grateful for the time she had been given, but it was hard to get through each day. During our last summer visit, though, she was visibly more hopeful than I had seen her in some time, having just received a letter from Professor Moltmann, who was planning to visit her when he traveled to the United States in November. This news raised her spirits and gave her energy to return to the writings we first read together in my theology course.

Like me, Kelly had a conversion to hope after reading Professor Moltmann's theology for the first time. My conversion in graduate school gave me energy to actively work for real social change even when I am tempted toward despair. Kelly's conversion in prison gave her a new sense of purpose and direction, even and especially in the face of death. "For a while now, and because I was on death row, I didn't have a plan for my life," she shared in her graduation speech, "but I now have a plan."

> The greatest journey I've ever taken is through the theology program, which has affected all aspects of my life. Now I can do nothing but obtain all the knowledge I can through the Bible, theology, and great theologians like my friend Dr. Moltmann. . . . This journey will never end, and I've come to a point in my life where I've found out who I am, where I'm hoping to go, and what direction to take. In the theology program, I found people, my fellow students and instructors, who are on that same journey.

As we awaited the next death warrant, which would come just a few weeks later in early fall, we invited others to join us in this journey of reflection and action through the hashtag #theologyofhope. On both sides of the ocean, professors engaged seminarians and graduate students in reflections on hope in light of Kelly's pending execution. Every day on Facebook and

141. Griffith, *Fall of the Prison*, 102, 106.
142. Douglass, *Narrative of the Life*, 85; King Jr., *Testament of Hope*, 299.

Twitter we paired insights from Professor Moltmann, like, "God's belief in us awakens our powers and gives us new ones we never dreamed of," with concrete actions: "We have the power today to fight this execution and be a voice for mercy. Call GA Board of Pardons and Paroles, 404–656–4661."

Our reason for reflecting on hope during that time may seem obvious. On the one hand, our hope was clear. We hoped for clemency, that Kelly's sentence would be commuted from death to life in prison without parole. On the other hand, what it means to be people of hope in the face of condemnation to death is not at all clear. For the threat and likelihood of death surrounded Kelly on every side. In the midst of this, Moltmann writes that we are tempted toward false certainties in one of two ways, each of which betrays the difficulty of hope and makes us passive. On the one hand, we are tempted toward the presumption that surely God will not let this happen, the execution was halted before, and if we keep the faith, we will get what we hope for. On the other hand, we are tempted toward despair that, surely, we will not. We presume that nothing we do will matter; the Georgia Board has spoken and they already denied Kelly clemency in February. In contrast to both of these temptations, biblical hope affords strength to live in the tension between false certainties. As we fought for Kelly's life, we had no certainty, only a command. We were to actively resist death-dealing powers and live into the promises of God. These promises include the kingdom come (Matt 6:10), the reconciliation of all things (Col 1:20), the total restoration of this world (Eph 1:10), and that nothing is lost (John 6:39)—all our energies are gathered like patchwork into the tapestry of God's restored world. Biblical hope demands that we live into the kingdom of God *now*—that we live into God's intended social order "on earth as it is in heaven"—as we fight present injustice, with confidence that when we do, we revolutionize and transform the present.[143] When we embody this hope, we protest against present injustice. We proclaim in a contrarian key that the way things are is not the way they have to be. A new world has come.

As it turned out, those months since the stayed execution had been for Kelly a garden of Gethsemane, a long, dark night of loneliness and anxiety, where it was hard for her to focus and hard for her to sleep. But when I spoke with Kelly in mid-September, the day after she received her second death warrant, she sounded strong. "I am determined," she said, "to make the most of every moment I have." That determination gave me permission to live fully in the present moment as well.

143. Moltmann, *Theology of Hope*, 16.

And we did, at her "death watch" visitation on Monday, September 28, as about twenty of us rotated in and out of the visitation space. The mood was celebratory—we were together in robust community—even as we awaited news about whether or not the Board would grant Kelly a second clemency hearing. I was sitting around the visitation table when a friend reminded Kelly of her favorite camp song, "Pharaoh, Pharaoh," sung at a Kairos retreat she did in prison. The two jumped out of their seats and sang, moves and all, "Pharaoh, Pharaoh, oh, baby, let my people go," ending the chorus with a playful, high-pitched "Free!" The officer in the back, charged with recording Kelly's every move, was writing furiously, and the four of us around the table were laughing hysterically, everyone so full of life. Kelly turned that space, called death watch visitation, into a song and dance of freedom.

Later in the visit, a seasoned death penalty abolitionist, Murphy Davis of the Open Door Community, relayed a message from a retired chief justice of the Georgia Supreme Court, Norman Fletcher, who had spoken a few nights before at an anti-death penalty banquet. He no longer supports the death penalty and told Murphy that he was wrong, on *legal* grounds, to deny Kelly's appeal when her case came before him in 2000. Kelly should have been spared, Judge Fletcher said, based on the disproportionate nature of her sentence when compared with her co-defendant.[144] "He's eaten up by his role in your pending execution and he's asked for your forgiveness," Murphy said. Kelly quickly responded, "Please tell him he is forgiven. I don't hold bitterness or hatred. I don't want him to carry this."

On the drive back from the prison in early evening, after saying my final goodbye, I got a call from Murphy. "Have you heard?" she asked in a tone I could not decipher. "The Board has granted a hearing." I wept with relief like Kelly had received clemency itself. A second hearing was extremely rare and it led us all to believe that the Board must be open to moving in a different direction.

On Tuesday morning, the day of the scheduled execution, I agreed to go on CNN later that afternoon to talk about Kelly. I was nervous not only about the interview but also that I might find out the news of the Board's decision while on national television. My friend Mary Catherine, who visits on death row and accompanied Marcus Wellons during his execution the year before, came with me to offer support. I was backstage in the makeup chair, having mascara applied, when she placed her hand

144. Cook, "Former Ga. Chief Justice Regrets Vote."

gently on my shoulder and told me the news that came through a text: "Clemency denied." Minutes later, I sat in front of the camera in grief and shock as I watched CNN anchor Brooke Baldwin read the statement from Doug's parents as it scrolled down the screen. "We along with our friends and supporters and our faith will continue fighting for Doug until he gets the justice he deserves," the statement read. "For those of us that loved him, we will always feel great sorrow and indescribable pain at how he was so brutally taken from us."[145] The anchor then asked if I had heard about Pope Francis's last minute appeal for Kelly. The Pope had been visiting the US the week before and had urged Congress to abolish the death penalty. In his letter, sent through his diplomatic representative, he wrote, "While not wishing to minimize the gravity of the crime for which Ms. Gissendaner has been convicted . . . and while sympathizing with the victims, I nonetheless implore you, in consideration of the reasons that have been presented to your Board, to commute the sentence to one that would better express both justice and mercy."[146] Brooke Baldwin then asked about Kelly's children.

That evening I learned that the Board made Kelly's three children choose between visiting their mother one last time or fighting for her at the second clemency hearing. They chose to fight. But once there, only the oldest son was permitted to speak. The Board had once before dismissed their plea that their mother be spared; now they silenced them altogether. More disturbingly, in the clemency application to the Board, Kayla had clearly stated that she would be revictimized by her mother's execution: "My dad would not want my mom to be executed, even knowing her role in his murder. He would not want us to endure another devastating loss. . . . My father's death was extremely painful for many people, but I've recently concluded that in many ways I was the person who was most impacted by his murder." And in a video we released a few weeks before, she added, "My brothers and I lost one parent, I don't know that I can lose another one. I don't know that I can handle that, because it is the most awful feeling, to know that they could both be gone."[147]

In the Family Restaurant at the truck stop across the street from Jackson prison, a small handful of us who knew Kelly well gathered with Kayla

145. Hicks, "Gissendaner Case Tests the Quality of Mercy"; Estep, "Family of Kelly Gissendaner's Slain Husband."

146. Cook, "Pope."

147. "Statement of Kayla Gissendaner." See also Casey and Bennett, "Clemency Application," 48.

for the night. Kelly could call her lawyers' cell phones and remained in touch throughout the evening. When all legal options had been exhausted and the United States Supreme Court denied the last appeal, Kelly called one final time. Kayla put her on speaker phone. We crowded around this little device held in the palm of her hand and heard Kelly sob as she grieved her own death. She wept, not only because she was rightfully scared in the face of so many botched executions, but also because she had so much to live for.[148] She wanted to live even as she had faith that God's mercy and love awaited her. Kelly dwelled to the end in biblical hope, a hope that does not give up on this life for something better beyond the grave, even if, Kelly made clear, this meant spending her days in the harsh and unforgiving confines of the prison. Instead, biblical hope affirms life in this world and seeks "the goodness of the Lord in the land of the living" as the psalmist sings (27:13)—a life in which she could continue her relationship with her adult children, her unique ministry to others in prison, her exploration of theology. Sobbing with her, we told her we loved her and that she wasn't alone. But every word felt inadequate, until Cathy, a priest and former theology instructor, shouted into the phone: "Kelly, you can do this. You can do this, Kelly."

"Let nobody rob you of your dignity; you are a beloved daughter of God," Professor Moltmann wrote to her in his last letter. "Those who want to take your life really don't know what they are doing. Forgive them; their future is dark. You are the truly free one."

Half an hour later, strapped to the cruciform gurney, as one condemned and free, Kelly sang "Amazing Grace" until the poison took her life. "There in the Georgia night, the amazing grace of Kelly Gissendaner was silenced," wrote *Chattanooga Times* columnist David Cook. "As children wailed in truck stop booths, the state-sanctioned machinery of death rolled through the Bible Belt night like an I-75 rig."[149]

Some minutes before, as she entered the death chamber sobbing, Kelly had addressed her last words to her pastor and lawyer, who sat behind glass watching the horror: "I love you, Sally. And I love you, Susan. You let my kids know I went out singing 'Amazing Grace.' And tell the Gissendaner family I am so sorry that amazing man lost his life because of me. And if I could take it back—if this would change it—I would have done it a long

148. For example, the year before there had been a string of three executions in Oklahoma in which the individuals were visibly seen agonizing in pain after the drugs were administered. In light of this, Kelly had said to me, "I'm not afraid of death but I am afraid of dying."

149. Cook, "The Amazing Grace of Kelly Gissendaner."

time ago. But it's not, and I just hope they find peace and I hope they find some happiness. God bless you."[150]

In a poem penned the next day on Facebook urging readers not to look away from the evil clearly on display, nor legitimate the horror by too quickly appealing to other-worldly comfort, a longtime death penalty abolitionist and theologian wrote, "I will not speak of resurrection for three days."

A few months later, I appeared with Professor Moltmann on a live podcast that was celebrating the fortieth anniversary of his book *The Crucified God*. I was asked what this book means to me in light of my experience with Kelly. I shared the vivid image of him signing Kelly's copy of *The Crucified God* inside the prison. The symbolism of that moment is as powerful to me as the story he tells in his autobiography of the book falling from the shelf of liberation theologian, Jon Sobrino, into a pool of blood after six Jesuit priests were slaughtered by the Salvadorian Army in 1989. Professor Moltmann's book speaks of a God in solidarity with those who suffer—in solidarity in a particular way with victims of state execution. The text bears witness to the God who absorbs the evil of state-sanctioned murder in God's very own body in order to condemn it and overcome it.

Professor Moltmann was then asked how we are to understand hope in light of Kelly's execution. His answer was firm and clear, pointing us to the work ahead. "Hope," he said, "is protest."

---

150. From CNN's coverage, audio of Kelly's last words at https://www.youtube.com/watch?v=99Waoz5ywt8.

Part 2

Letters and Papers from Prison: Correspondence with Jürgen Moltmann

The Beginning of Friendship

July 2010

Dear Mr. Moltmann,

First off let me say what an honor to be able to write you. You are one of my favorite theologians.

I also know Murphy Davis, Ed Loring, and Jennifer McBride. I have known Murphy and Ed for many years and Dr. Jennifer McBride is my theology teacher here at Metro State Prison, where I am the only female in the State of Georgia on death row. I've been on death row for eleven years, so it is also an honor and privilege to be able to be a part of the theology class, where I first learned of you and became a huge fan.

In theology class we just did a study on "Christian hope." When I did this study I had to ask myself 2 questions: 1) What is the Christian hope for individual persons? 2) What is going to happen to me and those whom I love? My answer is I believe in the resurrection of the body and life everlasting. Jesus promises every Christian the indwelling power of the Holy Spirit, to lead and reveal God's truth within me. God is made up of three persons: God the Father, Jesus the Son, and the Holy Spirit. I learned the word, "parakletos." This word signifies a comforter, a helper, an advocate and a counselor, as Jesus described. The Holy Spirit has led to a greater understanding of Gospel truths, given me strength to endure the hostility of the world, and helps me communicate with God.

I can't understand the ways and nature of God because I have been shaped by earthly circumstances. My mind has been, in a sense, grounded, and that grounding can lead me to death or a disconnection with God. Still, I desperately need a way to communicate with God. My earthly body and mind blocks me from intimacy with a holy, sinless God. The Holy Spirit helps me connect to God's ways—which are unreachable on my own.

The Holy Spirit has shown me the truth when the world offers lies and uncertainty. I am receptive to the Holy Spirit speaking to me through my spirit. The Holy Spirit has also spoken to me through other people, events and circumstances. I've tried to program my mind and body to detect, think, react and process the Holy Spirit's active voice and signs in my life as a Christian seeking a much deeper relationship with God.

The Holy Spirit not only gives me divine insight to help avoid unnecessary trouble in my life, the Holy Spirit is also my guide, dragging me back toward the image and likeness of God.

Without the Holy Spirit, I, with my own ability, am powerless to change. I had to accept the Holy Spirit's leading and power. And of course the complete fulfillment of this change will occur solely by the Holy Spirit in the next life. But, I can still discover what this means for me in my earthly life; the degree to which I follow the Holy Spirit's lead determines how far I'll get toward my goal here on earth of being transformed to God's image and likeness.

I was profoundly changed when I united myself with the Spirit of God who gives me the "freedom" to change in ways I can't even fully imagine right now.

This does not mean, of course, that I become Jesus, or that I become God. But, because the Holy Spirit dwells in me, I have access to all three aspects of the Holy Trinity. I have Jesus within me. I have God within me, which allows me the right to be called "child of God" and joint heir with Christ for what my Heavenly Father owns. Yes! As a believer, a child of God, there will come a day when we all will be able to share in all things.

Dr. Jennifer McBride jokingly calls me an "overachiever" ☺ in class. I don't know if I'd call myself an overachiever, but I'm very serious about this class, and anything that now has to do with theology.

Mr. Moltmann, I really hope to hear back from you when you have the time to write. I'd love to hear thoughts on what I've wrote on "Christian Hope."

Thank you for taking the time to read my letter.

Please be blessed and take care of you, always

With Deepest Regards—

Kelly R. Gissendaner

August 8, 2010

Dear Prof. Moltmann,

I am writing, first, to deliver a letter from Kelly Gissendaner, a student I have gotten to know well through a Candler-sponsored theology program for incarcerated women that I help direct. Kelly is the only woman on death row in Georgia. She is very interested in theology and admires your work, which we read in the theology foundations course I taught. I have apologized to her that it has taken me a good month to deliver this to you—I have been overwhelmed with summer teaching at Candler and revising my manuscript on top of my work at the prison, and I have wanted to include this letter with hers. With Kelly's permission, I am also sending you an essay she wrote on Bonhoeffer's *Life Together*. Since Kelly wrote this letter, the prison has gotten a new warden who has decided she can no longer participate in the program since she is on death row. This is a great disappointment for everyone—the teachers, students, and, of course, Kelly herself. It's been an honor to teach in this program and to learn from the theological reflections of students like Kelly.

I want to take the opportunity to give you an update since we last spoke in Prague in 2008. I now have a contract for *The Church for the World* with Oxford University Press and am turning in the revised manuscript in October. I wonder if you might consider offering an endorsement? I've spent the last year bringing to the surface the main argument, so while the content hasn't changed much since you last read it, the level of clarity and focus has. May I send you the revised manuscript in October?

I also want to share that some months after I moved to Atlanta, I took your advice and visited the Open Door Community. Ed and Murphy were excited to hear that you had directed me towards them! The Open Door has become my worshipping community for the past year and a half. Worshipping there was especially helpful as I transitioned from being a postdoc to beginning my work with the theology certificate program at the prison.

I am sending along my recently published, co-edited volume on Bonhoeffer and King. The introduction highlights the witness of the Open Door Community and the creative ways they carry on each of their legacies. At the American Academy of Religion in November, the Bonhoeffer Society will be hosting its annual dinner at Ebenezer Baptist Church. Are you planning to come to Atlanta?

I hope you are doing well and enjoying a pleasant summer in Tübingen.

Sincerely,

Jenny

Jenny McBride

Tübingen, August 30, 2010

Dear Ms. Kelly Gissendaner,

It was most kind of you to write and send me your letter. Thank you very much. I am deeply impressed by the theological ideas of your strong faith. May God's good Spirit embrace you and guard you always and inspire you. Theology is a great passion and a journey of adventures and discoveries in the holy mystery of God. I am glad you joined the "theology certificate program" of Jennifer McBride and found guidance and support in your searching for the truth.

I shall try to answer your 2 questions and try to do it on a personal level:

1. Christian hope for the individual persons: In traditional terms this is: Resurrection and Eternal life. In my explanation: The resurrections from the dead will happen immediately after death, or better in death. There is only one second between death and eternal life. "Today," not in three days, not at the end of days, but "today you will be with me in paradise," said the dying Christ on the cross. This is the "Today" of the eternal God, God's eternal presence. And we shall be saved and happy in God forever. Resurrection is the resurrection of life, not really of the "dead." The life we have lived from birth on in all the good and heavy moments will be raised, and when raised from death also healed from the wounds of life. "Resurrection" is the final healing process of our lives, just as Jesus is saying to the deeply bent down: Stand up, daughter of Zion. And if somebody would intervene: But is there not a final judgment of God?, I would answer: And the last word of the judge is: "Behold, I make all things new." Read Psalm 96 and 98 to see what will happen when the Lord comes and rejoices with heaven and earth.

2. But the hope for the coming of God and his new creation of all things is not only a personal one. Our personal hope is embedded in our universal hope, and our hope for the universe is: sin, lies and violence will disappear from the earth and peace and the righteousness of God will renew the earth. There is hope against the terror in this world. We shall never give up anything or anyone, but pray for them. Resurrection means also: Death will be no more, and the hell is broken, and the separation from God will disappear when God is coming to dwell in his earth forever. What we feel already

now as the Indwelling of the Holy Spirit, will fill the whole universe. The Spirit will be poured out on all flesh, and this is not only Christian flesh, but all of humanity, and not only human flesh, but all the living beings. "Kol basar" as the Hebrew word is, cf Gn 9, 10.

3. "What will happen to me?" Kelly, God has embraced you already, Jesus is with you and the Holy Spirit dwells in your heart: Nothing and Nobody can tear you from God's hands, for God is God. And the risen Jesus is waiting for you on the other side. You are expected. And eternal joy will be over your head forever.

If you pray, try the "Abba, dear father" prayer of Jesus, and you will feel how close Jesus and his God and the Spirit of Life is with you. It helped me very much to overcome the distance between heaven and earth, the Holy Spirit and my own spirit.

Please feel free to write again. Each letter of yours I am reading very carefully and with great sympathy.

Peace be with you and a strong Hope.

Yours ever,

Jürgen Moltmann

Tübingen, August 31, 2010

Dear Jenny (if I may),

Thank you for your letter and for the letter of Kelly Gissendaner. I was very moved by her letter and wrote an answer. I have sent my letter to the State Prison, and here is a copy for you in case the warden continues his antichristian behavior. Unbelievable!

I am very glad you found the Open Door community and they found you. I am admiring Murphy and Ed deeply for what they are doing and visit them whenever I am coming to Atlanta. I have no chance to come to AAR

[American Academy of Religion] meeting in November, because I hope to be in Beijing at that time. But there is a visit in planning for the fall of 2011, if God wills and I live. Will you stay at Emory?

Thank you for the book on Bonhoeffer and King. I would like to be with you at Ebenezer. In the early years I met Coretta King there.

When Oxford University Press is publishing your dissertation, I shall be happy to write a short blurb. Send the manuscript whenever you like. I may read it in December.

If you meet JoyAnn and Steffen give them my warm greetings and give my blessings to Murphy and Ed and the whole community at Ponce de Leon.

All good wishes,
Yours ever,

Jürgen

September 20, 2010

Dear Jürgen—(Mr. Moltmann)

It was so wonderful and an honor to hear back from you. Thank you so much for writing me back. I was <u>really</u> excited to receive your letter. No one understood my excitement and when I told Jennifer McBride she told me, "Sometimes being a theologian can be lonely." Boy, I'm learning that really fast! ☺

Jennifer said she told you that the new warden here at Metro pulled me out of the "theology certificate program." I was hurt and very upset— to say the least. Even though I can't go to class, class (the instructors) has been coming to me. I continue to do and turn in my work. What God has for me no one—not even the warden—can take it away.

Thank you for answering my 2 questions. I just did one of my final papers of this quarter of the theology program on the resurrection. I loved your insight about the "resurrection from the dead will happen immediately after death, or better in death." According to the New Testament, the resurrection of Jesus meant that he who gave himself as the Suffering Servant of God is now revealed to be the triumphant Lord. He who came preaching the kingdom of God is now seen to be the Sovereign King of the kingdom! The resurrection happened in this world. For Jesus himself and for us it means the renewal of human life, not escape from it. The resurrection, I believe, does not have to do only with the significance of Jesus for us after we die and leave this world. It has to do with our lives here and now, also.

But, should I believe what realized eschatology holds that the coming of Jesus and especially his resurrection means that the long hoped-for kingdom of God is a present reality, here and now?

The Gospels tell us that during his earthly ministry Jesus fed the hungry, defended the cause of the poor and outcast, healed the sick, raised the dead, comforted the sorrowing, forgave sinners and gave them a new start of life, demonstrated his power over evil spirits that "possessed" and destroyed the bodies, minds and souls of people. For the first Christians, Jesus' compassion for outsiders and his miracles were more than signs of his care for needy individuals; they were signs that the loving and just rule of God on earth was not just something to be expected in the distant or even near future but something that was happening before the very eyes of those who encountered him. Jesus' death and resurrection, then, were only the final confirmation of his kingdom—bringing life. In the earthly and risen Jesus, God's will was and is being done on earth as it is in heaven. In him God's Kingdom has already come and is a present reality for all who "have eyes to see and ears to hear." Those are just my thoughts.

You asked me to read Psalm 96 and 98. When God comes in the Bible God's justice is not something terrible to be avoided but a great blessing to be hoped for and received with joy and thanksgiving. This is why Calvin can say in Question 87 of the Geneva Catechism: "We should not then fear the last judgment and have horror of it? No, since we are not to come before any judge than he who is our advocate, and who has taken our cause in hand to defend us." God's justice is not a terrible alternative to God's love; it is God's love!

I could go on and on, but I won't take up any more of your time.

I hope you are enjoying Jennifer McBride's book. I've read the first 3 chapters and think it is awesome! I am supposed to receive the next 4 chapters this week, and I can't wait

I enjoy writing you, plus, again, it's such an honor. I look forward to hearing back from you.

Please take care of you and peace be with you always.

Yours truly—

Kelly

Kelly R. Gissendaner

20 Sept. 2010 Mon.

Dear Jürgen - (Mr Moltmann)

It was so wonderful, and an honor to hear back from you. Thank you so much for writing me back. I was really excited to receive your letter. No one understood my excitement and when I told Jennifer McBride she told me, "Sometimes being a theologian can be lonely". Boy, I'm learning that really fast! ☺

Jennifer said she told you that the new warden here at Metro pulled me out of the "Theology Certificate Program". I was hurt and very upset — to say the least. Even though I can't go to class, class (the instructors) has been coming to me. I continue to do and turn in my work. What God has for me no one - not even the warden - can take it away.

Thank you for answering my 2 questions. I just did one of my final papers of this quarter of the theology program on the Resurrection. I loved your insight about the "Resurrection from the dead will happen immediately after death, or better in death." According to the New Testament, the resurrection of Jesus meant that He who gave himself as

Letter from Kelly to Jürgen.

THE SUFFERING SERVANT OF GOD IS NOW REVEALED
TO BE THE TRIUMPHANT LORD. HE WHO CAME
PREACHING THE KINGDOM OF GOD IS NOW SEEN
TO BE THE SOVEREIGN KING OF THE KINGDOM.
THE RESURRECTION HAPPENED IN THIS WORLD.
FOR JESUS HIMSELF AND FOR US IT MEANS
THE RENEWAL OF HUMAN LIFE, NOT ESCAPE FROM
IT. THE RESURRECTION, I BELIEVE, DOES NOT
HAVE TO DO ONLY WITH THE SIGNIFICANCE OF
JESUS FOR US AFTER WE DIE AND LEAVE THIS
WORLD. IT HAS TO DO WITH OUR LIVES HERE AND
NOW, ALSO.

BUT, SHOULD I BELIEVE WHAT REALIZED
ESCHATOLOGY HOLDS THAT THE COMING OF JESUS AND
ESPECIALLY HIS RESURRECTION MEANS THAT THE LONG
HOPED-FOR KINGDOM OF GOD IS A PRESENT REALITY,
HERE AND NOW?

THE GOSPELS TELL US THAT DURING HIS
EARTHLY MINISTRY JESUS FED THE HUNGRY,
DEFENDED THE CAUSE OF THE POOR AND OUTCAST,
HEALED THE SICK, RAISED THE DEAD, COMFORTED
THE SORROWING, FORGAVE SINNERS AND GAVE
THEM A NEW START IN LIFE, DEMONSTRATED HIS
POWER OVER EVIL SPIRITS THAT "POSSESSED"
AND DESTROYED THE BODIES, MINDS AND SOULS

OF PEOPLE. FOR THE FIRST CHRISTIANS, JESUS'
COMPASSION FOR "OUTSIDERS" AND HIS MIRACLES
WERE MORE THAN SIGNS OF HIS CARE FOR NEEDY
INDIVIDUALS; THEY WERE SIGNS THAT THE loving
AND JUST RULE OF GOD ON EARTH WAS NOT
JUST SOMETHING TO BE EXPECTED IN THE DISTANT
OR EVEN NEAR FUTURE BUT SOMETHING THAT WAS
HAPPENING BEFORE THE VERY EYES OF THOSE WHO
ENCOUNTERED HIM. JESUS' DEATH AND RESURRECTION,
THEN, WERE ONLY THE FINAL CONFIRMATION OF HIS
KINGDOM- BRINGING LIFE. IN THE EARTHLY AND
RISEN JESUS, GOD'S WILL WAS AND IS BEING
DONE ON EARTH AS IT IS IN HEAVEN. IN HIM
GOD'S KINGDOM HAS ALREADY COME AND IS A
PRESENT REALITY FOR ALL WHO "HAVE EYES TO SEE
AND EARS TO HEAR. THOSE ARE JUST MY THOUGHTS.
    YOU ASKED ME TO READ PSALM 96 AND 98.
WHEN GOD COMES IN THE BIBLE GOD'S JUSTICE
IS NOT SOMETHING TERRIBLE TO BE AVOIDED
AND DREAD BUT A GREAT BLESSING TO BE HOPED
FOR AND RECEIVED WITH JOY AND THANKSGIVING.
THAT IS WHY CALVIN CAN SAY IN QUESTION 87
OF THE GENEVA CATECHISM: " WE SHOULD NOT
THEN FEAR THE LAST JUDGMENT AND HAVE
HORROR OF IT? NO, SINCE WE ARE NOT TO

PAGE
4

Come before any judge than He who is our
advocate, and who has taken our cause
in hand to defend us." God's justice is
not a terrible alternative to God's love;
it is God's love!
     I could go on and on, but I won't
take up anymore of your time.
     I hope you are enjoying Jennifer
Mc Bride's "Book." I've read the first 3
chapters and think it is awesome! I
am suppose to receive the next 4 chapters
this week, and I can't wait.

     I enjoy writing you, plus. again. It's
such an honor. I look forward to hearing
back from you.
     Please take care of you and peace
be with you always.

                    Yours Truly -
                    Kelly R M
                    Kelly R. Gissendaner

Tübingen, November 20, 2010

Dear Kelly,

Friede sei mit Dir!

Thank you so much for your long letter of September 20. I am sorry to be so late in answering, but was on the way still lecturing in many countries with 84 years [of age]. Your letter is a great piece of theology. Congratulations! What you are writing on "resurrection" and the present relevance of this hope deserves the best grades in a doctoral seminar. You can teach! But apart from this quality your words are speaking to the heart. Try to tell it to others. Or write a longer article on this topic and give it to Jenny.

I think you have beautifully balanced the future and the present relevance of the kingdom of God. Your emphasis on what happens already here and now in this world in accepting the excluded, healing the sick and raising the downtrodden is important. What will happen after death is not only important for us personally but for those who have passed away and the past world. On this Sunday we are remembering the dead—for me they are the killed and murdered in World War II, where I survived as a [child] soldier and they not—we are remembering not only in sorrow, but also we hope in the common resurrection and the life of the world to come.

When you have a clear vision of the personal eschatology, look into the cosmic eschatology and study Colossians and Ephesians: Christ and the chaotic powers and the reconciliation of the cosmos. Think about the creation and the new creation. The category "new" is universal. This is not superfluous speculation but of eminent ecological relevance. Can I send you my book, "The Coming of God" (2000)?

We are going into the season of advent. This was always the most exciting time for me, as a child and now as an old man. It is the time to open one's heart for the coming of the Lord, or better: of the coming of the divine child. God as a newly born child. We may expect something great and significant, and God comes to us in the insignificant and the weak and the defenseless child in Bethlehem. When we embrace it he will embrace us.

I am sending you a little star made by refugee children from Zimbabwe in South Africa. All my good wishes and blessings are with you.

Yours ever,

Jürgen

{No date provided}

Dear Jürgen,

I hope this letter finds you well rested after lecturing in many countries. I do think you are amazing to still be lecturing and sharing your wisdom and knowledge with so many others. For those who hear you I know that's a blessing to them. If I ever get the opportunity to just meet you I would be in awe. To be able to sit down and have a conversation with you would be truly amazing!

I am going to write a longer article on the resurrection and give it to Jenny. I was wondering what you thought of Jenny's book? I thought it was really well written and an amazing work of theology. I really enjoyed reading the manuscript. And I'm blown away and humbled that my name is in the acknowledgements.

Speaking of books, yes, I would love for you to send me your book "The Coming of God." I ask just one favor—will you please sign it for me? I can't wait to read it! I am excited and can't think of a better Christmas gift. ☺ Thank you ahead of time.

I am going to start studying Colossians and Ephesians. I haven't started yet because I had to finish two final papers and a major project for the theology class. For my first major project I did a 3 month devotional—which I'd love for you to read—only if you have time. The title is "A Journey of Hope: Walking on the Road to Emmaus with Jesus."

The God in whom I hope is a God who not only will be but is powerful and a compassionate Creator and ruler of the world. The Crucified and Risen Christ who will come to overthrow all the powers of darkness and evil that spoil God's good creation and human life in it has already triumphed over them and even now is at work to complete the work he has begun. The reconciling and liberating Spirit whom God will pour out on "all flesh" (Joel 2:28) is already "blowing where it will" also outside the little circle of Christians in the world. I believe in the sovereign power and love of a God who is the world's creator. So I hope my words in my devotional will help achieve a little more humanity in a world that will not only be but is God's world.

We cannot have faith and hope in either secular or Christian programs and organizations that seek to solve all the word's problems. But if we believe in a living Lord and a life-renewing Spirit who are present and at work in the world here and now (even where they are not recognized and acknowledged) we can and should join forces with all people of good will who seek to alleviate human suffering and restrain the destructive power of hatred, greed, and oppression. Hope in the triune God means that we will expect and work for preliminary signs of the new humanity and new world that we know will surely come.

On that I will close. I hope your holidays are filled with many blessings, as well as your new year.

Yours truly,
Kelly

P.S. The prison would not let me have the little star made by the refugee children of South Africa. I am very heartbroken!

March 30, 2011

Dear Jürgen—

glücklich Geburtstag!

I know your birthday isn't until the 8th of April and by the time you receive this letter I hope it will be close to the 8th of April.

I was going to write you before this but was trying to wait until I was moved. The prison I'm in is closing. I was hoping to have a new address by the time I wrote you. Everyone was supposed to be gone from here by the first of April—but that is not going to happen. I am truly ready to leave this "snake pit"! At the prison I will be going to I am praying to be able to get back in theology classes. That is my number 1 goal! We will also be having our graduation for our theology class at the other prison we are going to. I am speaking at that graduation and I am excited. I have been working on what I'm going to say and some of what I want to say has been inspired by your autobiography "A Broad Place," which I just finished reading and have been touched in so many ways by your autobiography. I will get back to "A Broad Place" before I end this letter.

Right now I want to thank you for the beautiful postcard.[151] I want to also thank you for "The Coming of God" you had your publisher send. I <u>did</u> <u>not</u> get the small book you sent. The prison would not let me have it. My daughter packed it up during one of our visits. I would love to have the book and if you sent it to Jenny McBride she could get it to me.

I got "A Broad Place" for my birthday, which was the 8th of March. First off to learn you were a prisoner of war was sad, for so many reasons. The two things you said that really hit me are on page 27. The first is "I can still hear the screams of their victims echoing through the hut." And the 2nd was "I still have the scars to keep me from forgetting that time." While I was in the Army I also witnessed death and I too can still hear the screams. I also have scars, few are physical, a lot more are mental, from my life.

I love how you said that you decided <u>again</u> and <u>again</u> in specific terms for the discipleship of Christ when the situations were serious and it was necessary. And how Jesus sought you and found you. And that he came to you when you were lost. (page 30)

This really hit home, "Jesus' godforsakeness on the cross showed me where God is present—where he was in my experiences of death, and where he is going to be in whatever comes. Whenever I read the Bible again with the searching eyes of the Godforsaken prisoner I was, I am always assured

151. This postcard, as well as Kelly's copy of *The Coming of God*, are missing from the items she sent home. Therefore, the postcard is not included here.

of its divine truth." (page 31) I can relate to this, especially by saying, "the Godforsaken prisoner I am."

Then I got to part 4 "Theology of Hope" (which I have read about 5 times now) and now have a deeper hope than I ever thought I could have within these prison walls! So, thank you!

On a piece of paper, that I now carry in my pocket, it says:

"Common to all these new beginnings was hope:
with the power of hope one can let go of the old
and begin something new. At that time 'the knowledge
that there can be change' counted as 'the reasonableness
of hope.' We (I) sought out changes for the better because
we (I) expected the good." (page 100)

I read that every day. It has become a sort of prayer for me.

It's like I said, so much in your book touched me, opened my eyes, and taught me. And I could go on and on from page to page and point out those many things but then I would never finish this letter. Of course, there is one last page I do want to touch on. Page 350, it is your answer to a passage in Augustine's Confessions. It is beautiful! And it caused tears in my eyes! Your words are some of the most beautiful words I have read in a very long time—if ever. Thank you for sharing those words!

As we approach Good Friday and Easter many thoughts are on my mind. Questions, as well as answers. A few of those are: Is life absurd or does it have a purpose? And Jesus replies that not only do our lives have purpose but God has directly intervened in human affairs to make abundantly clear what that purpose is. What is the nature of ultimate reality? Jesus responds that the really real is generous, forgiving, saving love. In the end will life triumph over death? With unshaken confidence Jesus answers, the kingdom of my Father cannot be overcome, even by death. In the end everything will be alright. Nothing can harm you permanently; no loss is lasting, no defeat more than transitory, no disappointment is conclusive. Suffering, failure, loneliness, sorrow, discouragement, and death will be part of your journey, but the kingdom of God will conquer all these horrors. No evil can resist hope and grace forever.

On that I will close this so I can get it in the mail and on its way to you.

ad majorem Dei gloriam

Yours Truly—
Kelly

P.S. I've enclosed a picture I did. It's for your birthday. And I've enclosed a poem that was inspired by you.

Colored pencil drawing Kelly sent Jürgen. (Included with March 30 letter.)

Jürgen—

Happy Birthday!

This is a copy of a picture I did for my grandmother and wanted to share it with you for your birthday!

Dieu vous garde –

Kelly
2011

{Additional comments}
Youth is not a period of time. It is a state of mind, a result of will. A person doesn't grow old because they have lived a number of years. A person grows old when they desert their ideal. The years may wrinkle their skin, but deserting their ideal wrinkles their soul. Preoccupations, fears, doubts, and despair are enemies which slowly bow us toward earth and turn us into dust before death. You will remain young as long as you are open to what is beautiful, good and great; receptive to the message of others, of nature, of God.[152]

{Enclosed poem}

March 2011

"Why Me Lord?"

Who am I Lord
Who am I to be
Why on earth did you not destroy me
arrogant and puffed up I was
My ignorance as filthy as mud
You patiently looked at me each day
and watched as I walked the widened way
sinkin' in the crowd
as I sway in my own vile
Then in a micro of a second you looked down at me
and stuck your arm out for me to see
I grabbed hold of your unchanging hand

152. In this prose poem to Jürgen, Kelly draws on "Youth," by Samuel Ullman (1840–1924), written in 1918 when Ullman was seventy-eight. In his May 3 letter, Prof. Moltmann assumes Kelly is paraphrasing words from Albert Schweitzer.

leading me through the narrow road not quicksand
As I left some others behind
I didn't look back because I knew I'd be fine
Well dear Lord could I ask a question would you mind
Tell me anything my child you are mine can't you see
O Lord why did you save me
I thought it destiny for me to fall
Oh no my child your destiny is my royal hall
As I reign a thousand years and stop all the tears
But I didn't understand why did I choose the gate with the crowd
My child I called you but the noise was too loud
Why O Lord didn't you tell me before I entered the wrong gate
You would have not have believed that narrow was your gate and escaped
You saw much demise
and now appreciate all that I have for you to know my way is wise
You will love me more because I forgave you for all the wicked things you
    have done
If I'd changed your gate early on you wouldn't understand the plan I've
    formed
See my child I called you to be
exactly like the one you see

Tübingen, May 3, 2011

Dear Jenny,

Kelly Gissendaner asked me to send the next letter to her and also to you.
She was transferred to another prison. You may know where this is and
visit her.

This is however a good chance to write to you also. Congratulations that
you found a home and a good place with Murphy and Ed at the Open
Door Community. I was always admiring them and visited the Community whenever I came to Atlanta. Don't forget theology: I believe you have
something to say. The teaching in prisons is one of the best schools to teach
what really matters, and we can learn from the prisoners. Kelly Gissendaner
is amazing. Her letters to me are full of wisdom.

Elizabeth and I are coming to Emory October 24–29. I hope to find time to visit Kelly, but I don't know where Alto is located. We may perhaps go together.

Give my warmest greetings to Murphy and Ed. They are always on my mind, and take good care of yourself.

Warm greetings,

Jürgen

Tübingen, May 3, 2011

Dear Kelly,

It was a wonderful surprise to receive your birthday greetings and your beautiful drawing and the very true sentences of Albert Schweitzer of the youth of the mind. I thank you wholeheartedly. You are a good artist. Is this a picture of the church in your home? Anyway, I am sending as my reply a picture of the pulpit in the medieval church at the center of Tübingen, where I used to preach for the students during my active time as their professor.

You have read my autobiography "Broad Place" and your response with your life and death experiences is very moving for me. Thank you for your open-mindedness. Where have you been in the army? Was it Afghanistan? I hope you received the booklet I have sent to you. The title is "God Experiences." Your daughter will give it to you, because it was my last copy.

Your poem "Why me Lord?" is speaking to my heart and gives me much consolation. Thank you for sharing this with me. I shall treasure it.

I am sure the great light of Easter and Resurrection is shining into your place and fills your life with deep joy and the all-embracing hope.

Yours truly,

Jürgen

Jürgen Moltmann

Tübingen, July 15, 2011

Dear Jenny,

Greetings from old Tübingen! Thank you for your fax letter of July 7. I am glad to hear some good personal news from you. Congratulations for your call to Wartburg College, and also good wishes for your Oxford book. It is an excellent idea to write a "theological memoir" on your experiences at the Open Door community and at the prisons, thanks to Charles. Theology must be "lived theology." We learned this from Bonhoeffer. You must tell me about the Department of Correction forms you had to sign.

I am free on Friday, October 28, to go with you to Arrendale. Thank you for coming down to Atlanta for this. I appreciate this very much. I hope to find the right words in the service for the graduation of the class of 2010. You will certainly also speak, I suppose. I am looking forward to seeing Kelly face to face, but I hate prison systems!

By the way, my first name is not "professor."

Warm regards and all good wishes,

Jürgen

July 25, 2011

Dear Jürgen—

I do apologize for taking so long to write back. It has been harder than I thought it would be to get refocused and settled in a different prison. This was a huge change for me since I'd been at Metro for over 12 years. I am still not where I want to be thought wise. But I am getting there.

I have reread your book "A Broad Place" to help me get settled again.

91

I hear you are coming to the U.S. in October. And it would be a huge honor if I could meet you. I think I'd be speechless—and that would be a first for me. ☺

Either this Friday or the next I will be able to attend theology class once again. I will have class by myself away from the other students, but I will take what I can get for now. I was asked what I wanted to study and have requested a study on your book "Theology of Hope." I am looking forward to reading and studying your work. Hope plays a <u>huge</u> part in my life here and has since I have been on death row.

It is the good news of hope for the future even when my personal experience and world history seem to say there is no hope. I know Christian hope for individuals is hope in the God who raised Jesus from the dead; it is therefore hope for my own resurrection—hope for "the resurrection of the body" and "the life everlasting." Hope is a beautiful and amazing thing.

I wrote a poem I want to share with you. It's called "Can You Understand Me."

If you cannot trust in the Lord, you will not
be able to acknowledge my true heart

If you do not believe in the Word of the Lord
you will not understand my walk

If you are always worrying about the troubles
in your life you will not realize why I smile so often

If you cannot forgive your fellow human beings
you will not be able to perceive the love I feel

If you do not have real faith in the Lord
you will unequivocally not understand me

If you allow hatred supremacy in your heart and
mind you will not comprehend my joy and happiness

If you cannot trust your life in the hands of
the Lord you will not be able to know my peace

If you cannot put the Lord first in your life it
will be impossible for you to perceive the concept of my life

If you cannot believe in the power of the Lord
you have no chance in understanding me

If you cannot accept Jesus Christ as your Savior
you will never comprehend my faith

Can you understand me?

I hope to hear from you soon. Take care of you, and God bless.

Your friend—
Kelly

September 21, 2011, 7:00 PM

{Postcard}

Dear Kelly,

At this day and hour I remember you and embrace you in my prayer. Jesus is carrying you in his hands. I am grateful for your letter of July 25 and I am still admiring the picture you have drawn for me. Beautiful!

I am looking forward to visiting you on October 28! Jenny McBride will drive me and accompany me. I think I understand you with my heart.

Always your brother,

Jürgen

September 21, 7pm
2011

Dear Kelly,
at this day and hour I
remember you and
embrace you in my prayer.
Jesus is carrying you in his
hands. I am grateful for your
letter of July 25 and I am
still admiring the picture
you have drawn for me.
Beautiful!
I am looking forward to
visiting you on October 28!
Jenny McBride will drive
me and accompany me.
I think I understand you with
my heart. Always you
brother   Jürgen

STIFT URACH
Einkehrhaus der Ev. Landeskirche in Württ.
Telefon 07 125 / 94 99-0.
Bismarckstraße 12
72574 BAD URACH

Postcard from Jürgen to Kelly.

Theology Graduation Speech
Kelly Gissendaner

Today I feel like we have come full circle. When the class of 2010 started the Certificate in Theological Studies, Mrs. Seabolt was warden at Metro State Prison; and today as we graduate, it's with Mrs. Seabolt as warden of Lee Arrendale.

Some of you may be asking, "What is theology?" Theology is a study of God. You may also be asking, "Who is a theologian?" My pen pal and friend Dr. Moltmann says in his autobiography, *A Broad Place*, that "theology is a task for the whole people; every Christian is a theologian."

As I studied the doctrines in biblical and theological courses, my task was to ask at every point what the doctrines had to say about my social as well as my devotional life, my everyday private and public worship, my life here and now as well as my life in the "world to come." Only when I asked these questions could I fulfill the task of a good theologian—one who speaks and thinks about both the true God and real human beings in the real world.

From the start of the theology class I felt this hunger. Never have I had a hunger like this. I became so hungry for theology, and what all the classes had to offer, you could call me a glutton. I've now added in thirst for the accomplishment of my dream to continue the study of theology.

There came a time when I thought the whole theology program would be pulled from me. Let me explain. I am in a very unfortunate situation, not only here at Arrendale, but also in the state of Georgia. My reality is that I'm the only female on Georgia's death row; and while Warden Seabolt was at Metro State Prison, she gave me the opportunity to be a part of this wonderful theology program. Six months into the program, Warden Seabolt left Metro to a whole new administration. And my worst fears became my reality—I was pulled from the theology program. I was taken from my theological community. Being pulled from the program devastated me as badly as if someone had just told me one of my appeals had been turned down.

Since I couldn't go to the theology class, the theology classes came to me. The instructors came to me. Still, this was far from being in an ideal situation because now I had to have class and community through a gate. It was hard and most of the time frustrating, but I pushed on. I pushed on because of that hunger. I missed my fellow theology students and the bond we shared.

That gate at Metro was meant to keep everyone and everything separated from me. But that gate couldn't keep out the knowledge that I was so hungry for, nor friendship and community. And it sure couldn't keep out God.

The theology program has shown me that hope is still alive and that, despite a gate or a guillotine hovering over my head, I still possess the ability to prove that I am human. Labels on anyone can be notoriously misleading and unforgiving things. But no matter the label attached to me, I have the capacity and the unstoppable desire to accomplish something positive and to have a lasting impact.

As Genesis 1 reminds us, everything God made is good and has a purpose. I have become acutely aware, through Biblical and Theology Foundations, of a much greater purpose than my confinement, because of a spiritual yearning and ability to connect to theology.

Theology is about growing in truth, rather than being a finished thing. Even prison cannot erase my hope or conviction that the future is not settled for me, or anyone. History is still in the making. I have learned not to place my hope in all kinds of fantastic predictions and speculations about a future I cannot really know anything about. I have placed my hope in the God I now know, the God whose plans and promises are made known to me in the whole story of the life, death, and resurrection of Jesus Christ.

What we can all look forward to is not destruction, but the renewal of the life of our created world and our lives in it. We must remember that the clearest hope about what is going to happen in the future is what God has been doing in the past.

The greatest journey I have ever taken was not a physical journey. It was a spiritual and mental journey through the theology program that has affected all aspects of my life. This journey will never end, and I've come to a point in my life where I've found out who I am, where I'm hoping to go, and what directions to take. In the theology program, I've found people, my fellow students and instructors, who are on that same journey.

Each Friday for the first six months that I attended the Biblical and Theology Foundations classes, it all made me rethink and reevaluate my visions of life and, in turn, gave me a clearer way of seeing things in general, to think outside the box. For a while now, and because I am on death row, I didn't have a plan in my life, but thanks to the theology course and the wonderful instructors, I now have a plan. Now I do nothing but obtain all the knowledge I can through the Bible, theology, and great theologians like my friend Dr. Moltmann, so I can better my chances at being who I need to be. Just believing things are subject to change has propelled me to reach where the earth appears to meet the sky. When I seize that spiritual and mental posture, my negative situation cannot help but change. Through this transformation, I have taken a gradual course of action. The expectation is—this too shall come to pass.

To the Class of 2011:

I challenge you to step up the next level of your character, growth, and development. In your pit, or prison, receive the word and revelation and act on it; your life will never be the same. I implore you not to allow prison to rob you of your dream or vision, nor of your dignity or self-worth.

In all of us, there are untapped abilities. I encourage you to write that book, start that ministry, teach, study, pursue your dream.

Know that suffering can be redeemed. There is only one who can bring a clean thing out of something unclean, or turn a tragedy into a triumph, and a loser into a winner. When this miracle occurs, and only through Divine grace, our life is not wasted. When blind eyes are opened, then we will all see the greater purpose.

Let us put off hatred and envy and put on love and compassion. Every day.

By Kelly Gissendaner, October 28, 2011

Jürgen Moltmann
October 28, 2011

Dear Sisters and Brothers in Christ,

You have invited me to your Graduation Ceremony of the class of 2010. I am very grateful and happy to be here with you this morning. It is for me not only a privilege but also a precious gift. Your community is important for me. Therefore, I came.

You will receive today your Certificates in Theological Studies. When I first heard of your study of theology in prison, pictures of my youth and of the beginning of my own theological studies emerged from the depth of my memory. Yes, I remember: My theological studies started in a poor Prisoner-of-War-Camp after World War II. I was 18 years old when I became a Prisoner-of-War (POW) for more than 3 years. I was lucky: it was in Britain not in Siberia! In a camp of forced labor in Kilmarnock, Scotland, I read for the first time in my life the Bible and encountered Jesus. I had not decided for Christ, but I am certain Christ found me there when I was lost in sadness and desperation. He found me, as Christ has come to seek what is lost. I tried to understand what had happened to me. We had a "Theological School behind barbed wire." This camp was like a monastery. Excluded from time and world, imprisoned professors taught imprisoned students free theology. We studied Bible, church history and theology, but we also tried to come to terms with our death-experiences at the end of the war. Theology was for us at that time an existential experience of healing our wounded souls. These were the beginning of my theological studies and my first experiences of the Church of Christ, the Church in Prison Camps. Later I became a pastor and a professor of theology, but deep in my heart there is still sitting a frightened and sad POW.

I think this was always the case with the Church of Jesus Christ: There is the Church in the World and here is the Church in Prison. There is the Church in Society and there is the Church in the monastery. And this dual existence is also true for the experience of God. There are God-experiences on the way outside and there are God-experiences on the way inside.

On the way inside we are seeking God in the recognition of our inner self. There is a ring around God and the Soul. The more we recognize ourselves we recognize God. And the more we recognize God we recognize ourselves. Why? Because we are the "image of God." On the way outside we are seeking God in other human beings, because whatever they are they are images of God too. And we are seeking God in the beauties of God's creation and in the suffering of our fellow-creatures.

The way outside into the blessings and the troubles of the world is dangerous and adventurous as we surely all know. But the way inside is as dangerous and adventurous, full of temptations and blessings, because the soul is a broad place and a rich land. Teresa of Avila went this way and told us in her book "The Inner Castle" and Thomas Merton in our time went this way and told us in his "Seven Story Mountain" what he experienced in the monastery in Gethsemani, Kentucky.

When did Christians start to seek God on the way inside? It [was] the so-called "Desert Fathers," in fact young men from villages in Egypt in the 4th century. They wanted to follow Jesus into the desert. The first was a young man named Antonius. The desert was in old Egypt not the home of the gods, but the land of death and demons. Antonius lived in a cave in the desert, fought for his survival, fought against the demons, fought against his anxieties and saw the victory of Christ: "Death, where is your sting? Hell, where is your victory?!" as the apostle Paul quoted in the first Christian Easter hymn. Hundreds of young men followed Antonius, until an ex-soldier, a veteran came, his name was Pachomisch, and built the first Christian monasteries and brought discipline to the wild "Desert boys." The God-seeking Christians lived no longer in natural caves, but in man-made cells. Since that time, we have the dual formation of Christianity.

Monastery and world Christianity, monastic theology and world theology, the way inside and the way outside, the Church in Prison and the Church in the World. And both need each other.

You will receive your Certificates in Theological Studies today. Let me say a word to what "theology" is: "I believe in order to understand," is a famous characteristic of theology. The Monk-Father Anselm of Canterbury told us this. To believe is good—to understand is better.

Why is especially the Christian faith pressing for understanding? I think because for a Christian, faith is only a beginning of a new world. It is a longing for God and a desire to see the truth face to face.

> "For now we see through a glass, darkly,
> but then face to face;
> now I know only in part,
> but then I shall know
> even as also I am known" (1 Cor 13:12).

Christian faith is no blind fall, but a faith with open eyes. We pray with open eyes. We are not always happy with what we see here. All the more are we longing to see through the horizon of this world into the shining face of the Coming God. God has seen us already and will never let us out of his eyes. Therefore, the desire is in us to see God face to face and "enjoy him forever." Theology has only one problem: God. God is our pain—God is our joy—God is our longing. We are theologians for God's sake. Every Christian who believes and understands is a theologian, not only the professionals at Candler or Tübingen, every Christian!

Allow me to congratulate you: You are really theologians, and in fact excellent theologians. I have read a paper Jenny McBride has sent me, and I was impressed. My students at Tübingen could not have made it better. I would like to encourage you: Go on and take the next course in Theological Studies. And you must not only learn from other theologians, develop your own thoughts. We need your spiritual insights and theological reflections. There is a world-wide fellowship of all theologians. There is an age-old community of all theologians. Augustine and Thomas Aquinas, Martin Luther and Dietrich Bonhoeffer are our brothers and sisters in the Spirit of God. We need you: The theology in the world needs the theology in prison. The way outside would become a wrong way without the way inside. Without self-experience, there is no experience of God. You are the Church! We are sisters and brothers in Christ Jesus.

Friede sei mit Euch!

Jürgen Moltmann, Kelly Gissendaner, and Jenny McBride at the theology graduation.

Kelly giving Jürgen her theology capstone project, a devotional she wrote.

Kelly celebrating with theology certificate graduates.

Graduating students listening to Moltmann's speech.

Kelly with children, Kayla and Dakota, December 2013.

Kelly hugging daughter at graduation reception.

Jürgen Moltmann speaking with theology student.

Letters after Meeting

Tübingen, November 7, 2011

Dear Kelly,

Friede sei mit Dir!

Friday Oct 28 was for me the most important day of my visit to America this time. I was deeply impressed by your Graduation Ceremony in the little church behind the huge barbed wire and I am more than grateful to have shared this hour with you. A special gift was the hour with you and Jenny and to listen to you. Now I can better imagine you and your situation and your experiences inside and outside, when I think of you and pray for you. Looking at the graduates of 2010 I felt how important you are for them. You looked like a pastor for them and they were admiring you with their eyes. You are their older sister, if I may say so. Your "student remark" was very moving and touched my heart. Are you keeping a diary? I think many would like to know about your experiences and your courage to be in what you have gone through. To write things down is sometimes healing the soul. I shall never forget what I have seen and heard in your place. I returned with deep doubts about the whole prison system in your country and in mine.

Thursday Oct 27 was a kind of homecoming for me at Candler School of Theology, Emory University. I gave the Reformation Day Lecture and embraced many good old friends. On Wednesday Oct 26 I was—as always when I am coming to Atlanta—in the Open Door Community with Murphy Davis and Ed Loring. I think you know them. We had a very lively conversation with the volunteers and members of that community. I came there first on a rainy day in 1983 and since then every time. On Sunday Oct 30 I was home again in Tübingen where our daughter Susanne took care of my wife Elisabeth, who could not join me because she felt too weak.

I am sending you with this letter my "theological reflection" on Graduation day. And I am waiting to get your "student remarks." Please.

Forgive this typed letter. My handwriting is deteriorating because of my age.

Kelly, I am proud and happy to know you, I embrace you as your brother and friend,

Jürgen

Dear Kelly,

    Friede sei mit Dir !
Friday Oct 28 was for me the most important day of my visit
to America this time. I was deeply impressed by your Graduation Ceremony in the little church behind the huge barbed
wire and I am more than grateful to have shared this hour
with you. A special gift was the hour with you and Jenny and
to listen to you. Now I can better imagine you and your
situation and your experiences inside and outside, when I
think of you and pray for you. Looking at the graduates
of 2o1o I felt how important you are for them. You looked
like a pastor for them and they were admiring you with their
eyes. You are their older sister, if I may say so. Your
"student remark" was very moving and touched my heart.
Are you keeping a diary ? I think many would like to know
about your experiences and your courage to be in what you
have gone through. To write things down is sometimes healing the soul. I shall never forget what I have seen and
heard in your place. I returned with deep doubts about
the whole prison system in your country and in mine.
    Thursday Oct 27 was a kind of homecoming for me at Cand-
ler School of Theology, Emory University. I gave the Refor-
mationsday-Lectrueg and embraced many good old friends. On
Wednesday Oct 26 I was - as always when I am coming to
Atlanta - in the Open Door Community with Murphy Davis and
Ted Loring. I think you know them. We had a very lively conversation with tne volunteers and members of that community.
I came there first on a rainy day in 1983 and since then
every time. On Sunday Oct 3o I was home agagin in Tübingen
where our daughter Susanne took care of my wife Elisabeth,
who could not join my because she felt too weak.

Letter from Jürgen to Kelly.

I am sending you with this letter my "theological reflection" on Graduation day. And I am waiting to get your
"student remarks". Please.
Forgive this typed letter. My handwriting is deteriorating
because of my age.
   Kelly, I am proud and happy to know you, I embrace you
      as your brother and friend

Tübingen, November 7, 2011

Dear Jenny,

I just wrote a letter to Kelly, and this must be followed by a letter to you: Thank you so much to have taken me to that place. I was deeply impressed by the ceremony and by your theology in prison program and my deepest impression was Kelly herself: What a lively person, and what a "courage to be" in such a life-denying situation! On the return flight to Germany I got serious doubts about our prison systems, they are doing no one anything good.

Congratulations and warm greetings on your first academic position. The march into the promised land always begins in a desert; mine was the village of Wasserhorst, yours is at least surrounded by cornfields! Take your chance!

Enclosed you will find my address at the ceremony in the prison, where I was so beautifully introduced by you.

   Good wishes and blessing,
   yours ever,

   Jürgen

November 29, 2011

Jürgen—

It was so good to receive your letter. Thank you so much for the copy of your speech. I am enclosing a copy of my graduation speech along with a copy of the article that was done by Paul Wallace at Emory. Everything underlined in pink are my quotes.

Have you had the opportunity to read the devotional I wrote? I can't wait to hear your thoughts on my devotional.

It was a true honor to meet you and to be able to spend that extra time with you and Jenny. Graduation was an amazing day. I will never forget that day, or my time with you.

I don't keep a diary, but I do write my thoughts and feelings down. Most of the time those thoughts and feelings come out in the form of poetry. And that has been healing for my soul.

Yes, I do know Murphy and Ed. Murphy use to visit me when I first came to prison. I think the world of Murphy.

I hope your wife, Elisabeth, is feeling much better. Please give her my regards.

I wish more people had deep doubts about the prison system—all over the world. But so many are on the "lock them up and keep them" thinking that they can't see the forest for the trees.

I believe there is a misunderstanding of "good" and "bad." Therefore there is a misunderstanding that heaven is the reward for being good and hell the punishment for being bad—like an eternal lollipop or eternal spanking promised good or bad children. But according to Jesus, the truth is just the opposite: Heaven is for sinners and hell is for "good" people. To whom did Jesus address gracious words of invitation and promise? To people who were obviously guilty sinners. And [to] whom did Jesus address his sternest warning and threats of hellfire and eternal misery? He almost never mentioned hell except when he spoke to the Scribes and Pharisees—the moral, religious, church-going people of his day who wanted above all else to preserve the "moral values" and "religious traditions" of the day.

Anyway, we haven't received the pictures of graduation yet. But as soon as we do I will send you some copies. I can't wait to see them! I hope to get copies of those pictures soon.

I am so glad that we got the chance to meet—it means more to me than you know.

I embrace you as your sister and friend.

Kelly

Tübingen, December 10, 2011

Dear Kelly at Christmas:

Friede sei mit Dir! and may the Light of Christ illuminate the whole Ar-rendale Prison!

I am reading a piece of your "Journey of Hope by Faith" every morning. Your words are speaking to my heart. I am admiring your insights and thank God whenever I think of you.

Since visiting your "place" and meeting you personally I can better imagine what you are going through. I pray and hope for you.

Last week your letter of Nov 27 arrived with your graduation speech. Thank you so much. It was after all a very happy hour at lunch in your house behind that ugly barbed wire. I am still glad that you invited me.

I bless you and embrace you as your brother and friend,

Jürgen

1ˢᵗ Sunday
"LIGHT IN MY DARKNESS"

2 Corinthians 4:6 "For God, who said, "Let light shine out of darkness..." [NIV]

My childhood wasn't the greatest, but my world was anything but dark.

Then, something happened. My life bottomed out. Fast. Really fast. Light turned into darkness and then it was night for a really long time. After making one of the worst mistakes in my life, I was sent to live in a place where darkness is the norm. The only light I saw in here for the first years was an artificial light from the bright halogen lights; representative of man's pitiful attempt to overcome darkness.

Again, something happened. In the midst of the darkest dark I'd ever known, a real light began to shine, inside me, it seemed. If you are reading this try not to shut me out because I am writing from prison.

Don't be afraid of the dark. It's where the light will come to us. For the next couple of months, we'll spend time together and I'll try to describe how the light came - and continues to come - to me. I'm sure I'll come up short but, in a way, that's understandable. After all, how does one describe a miracle?

My Personal Notes:

_____

_____

_____

_____

_____

_____

_____

_____

_____

_____

_____

_____

_____

_____

_____

_____

_____

_____

A page from the devotional book Kelly wrote in the theology program.

8th Sunday
"ARRIVING AT METRO"

Joshua 1:9 "I hereby command you: Be strong and courageous; do not be frightened or dismayed, for the Lord your God is with you wherever you go." [NRSV]

It was a sunny day in November 1998, the 20th to be exact. I was close enough to the razor wire that I could see my distorted reflection in the tiny barbs. Handcuffed and shackled [my feet and hands connected to my midsection with chains], I was delivered to the care of the Georgia Department of Corrections. I was now the only female on Georgia's Death Row.

It's a gross understatement to say I was scared. I didn't think I would make it. I certainly didn't know God was with me. So, what did I do? Did I find a friendly face and confide in them? "Whew, I'm glad to see you. I guess I don't have to tell you how scared I am." No. Did I cry? No.

I puffed up my chest and acted like I wasn't scared. It was pretty easy. I'd been hiding my fear in one way or another for quite some time.

Years later, afraid and lonely, and tired of hiding it, I tentatively voiced my vulnerability to God. Since then, I've learned a little about courage and strength. It doesn't mean that I'm not ever frightened or dismayed; part of being strong and courageous is recognizing and admitting you're anything but. And, that you're not alone.

My Personal Notes:

_____

_____

_____

_____

_____

_____

_____

_____

_____

_____

_____

_____

_____

_____

_____

Page from devotional.

January 16, 2012

Dear Jürgen—

Thank you so much for your Christmas card! Instead of a card I did a "Christmas letter" this year and have enclosed a copy for you, even though it's a little late.

I also enclosed something I wrote on hope for theology class at the end of 2011.

I hope you are still enjoying my "Journey of Hope by Faith" devotional. I remember how much hard work I put into that devotional and how proud I am of it, even today.

Our meeting in October really touched my life in so many ways and I am so thankful that we got to meet and share such a special time together. As soon as I receive the pictures that were taken at graduation I would like to at least send you one of you and I—if you would like to have it.

That day still holds so many special memories for me. It's a time that helps me to pull through the tough times that are many here.

I'm going to keep this short, so I can get my writings in the mail to you. Your feedback means so much to me.

> Your Sister in Christ—
> Kelly

"Hope: The Theology of Despair"

The truth is that I am not an authority on hope. Until some years ago I didn't even know what hope was: I thought it was something akin to a wish, a pipe dream.

I was partly right. Hope is about wishing, but there's another element involved: expectation. Expectation that what we so fervently desire can be obtained. In a nutshell, to hope is to trust in the future as if it were a fountain of opportunity. But what if your past and present are mocking reminders that, too often, the viability of hope is determined by those events beyond your comprehension and control.

We are all children of ourselves. Who we are today—our attitudes, the nature of our perception about the world, about ourselves and the connection between them—[has] been produced by our responses to hope, and its shadowy counterpart, despair. The two cannot be separated. My great-grandmother came of age during the Great Depression. She was a cynic by necessity. Whenever someone spoke of hope she would give the same aphoristic response, "Hope in one hand and doo-doo in the other and see which hand gets the fullest the fastest." (Actually, she used a more colorful word than doo-doo.)

In retrospect, I can see that she was emphasizing the importance of spending more time actualizing our aspirations rather than vocalizing them. But, being a child, I received her words as affirming my growing [suspicion] that hope was no more valuable than, well . . . the "number two." It was a dark epiphany.

At the age of nine I adopted a new resolution to go with my epiphany: "Expect the worst and you will never be disappointed." This outlook on life bent my forced precocity into a warped shell—a shield I brandished like the head of Medusa, freezing all potential, all hope, into stone monuments of relinquished dreams. The years that followed were even more traumatic, life challenges that a lot of people endure and emerge victorious from. Me? It took time to recover hope. Actually, it took receiving time.

I am 43 years old. For the last 15 years of my life I have lived in the most hopeless place in the State of Georgia—Georgia's death row. In here the most oft-repeated axioms are "we can never win" and "they do what they wanna do"—"they" being those in positions of authority.

The one trait that most criminals share is hopelessness. Hopelessness is the root of all deviant behavior. Hopelessness tells us that the future is bleak, that all we have is the present moment. If our personality can be viewed as a chain of memories, hopelessness is the broken link that keeps us from even considering that we are larger than this moment, larger than these bodies, larger than our cultural and national identities. It cuts us off from the recognition that humanity, with all of its accomplishments and failures, is embodied in each person.

My hope was restored by degrees, and I did not do it alone. It has been a group effort. I have always felt part of the "interdependent web of existence of which we are a part." Knowing the truth about why I am in prison, it would be easy to give up hope, embrace bitterness and become what I was portrayed to be. But studying us—humanity—I know and am convinced that the only thing that separates angels from demons is that the latter gave up hope and in doing so came to personify hopelessness and all of its fruit. There can be no rehabilitation, no reform, without hope. Learning from my peers, from the great minds like Dr. Moltmann, gives me hope. Challenging those who work to keep me in prison, without resorting to lies and while maintaining my compassion, gives me hope.

Most of all, my mother's support and friendship, her strength and resilience, gave/gives me hope that I can live as courageously as she had in a life of adversity and struggle.

Hope, to me, is the mental, emotional and spiritual equivalent of that ineffable force that holds the universe together, and which has given the universe the ability to look upon itself through our eyes, and marvel at the breadth of its diverse and infinite beauty. Hope is not merely an attitude. It is our birthright.

Tübingen, February 10, 2012

Dear Kelly,

"Friede sei mit Dir"

I have not heard from you for quite a while. Did your situation change? Let me take part in your life and thinking. You are in my prayer every morning, and reading your "Journey of Hope by Faith" gives me much inspiration.

Can you continue your theological studies? Who is in charge now since Jenny left? I am still studying theology with 85 years and discover new ideas. It is an adventure of ideas, not only of faith. Theology is to love God with your mind.

Kelly, I remember you. Take good care of yourself and of your sisters in the house.

Yours ever,
Jürgen

March 5, 2012

Dear Jürgen—

I sent you a letter at the end of January with a paper that I'd wrote on hope for theology class. I'm guessing you never received that.

No, my situation has not changed, though my health has. I found out in January that I have lupus, which is an autoimmune disease. Then at the end of February I found out that I'm in the first stages of kidney failure. I have to start some medicine and it makes me feel tired most of the time. Other than that, I'm good.[153]

I am continuing my theological studies. Cathy Zappa has taken over for Jenny. Speaking of Jenny, she was just in Atlanta and I got to spend some time with her on Friday. It was <u>GREAT</u> to see her! I do miss her! She will be back for the summer and I look forward to spending some more time with her.

I have been researching some ideas for schools. I would <u>really</u> like to get my college degree. Ohio University seems like the best way to go. Now I have to come up with the money, which is really hard to do. For 8 hours, which is 2 classes, it's $1100.00 and for 20 hours its $2700, both include all books and materials. This is really a dream of mine now—I just don't know if I can make it happen, which is disappointing.

---

153. The lupus diagnosis turned out to be an error.

So, has your new book come out yet? I know when you were here you said you had a new one coming out. I can't wait to read it! I do look forward to reading it.

I'm enclosing 2 pictures for you. One is of you, Cathy Zappa (who took Jenny's place) and me. Then the other has Jenny and I, plus some others. I am still waiting on the one of you, Jenny and me. I will send you that one when I get it.

I will close this so I can get this to you. I will get another copy of my hope paper and send that to you also. Take care of you. And please write when you can.

Yours—
Kelly

Tübingen, March 12, 2012

Dear Kelly,

Thank you so much for your letter of March 5 and the photos. I am sorry to hear about your health problems. All this and that too. . . . It may become too much. Have patience with your body and yourself. Your body is your friend not your enemy. I am glad to hear that Jenny could visit you. I would like to do the same, but I am an old man now approaching the age of 86 (with two artificial joints in the knees and asthma), but I am still curious about the future here and there.

I must beg your pardon: I was out the country in February and found no time to answer your witness of hope. Now I am reading your words again and again and admire your insights and your courage. The last part belongs to the best I have read about hope. You know that I have gone through most parts of despair, knowing all cynicism about those who still expect and want something. In Latin however de-speratio comes from spes. Despair is the destruction of hope. Where there is no hope there is no desperation either. There is always some fire under the ashes. I learned that many disappointments are better than to give oneself up and condemn hope. Hope kept me alive and is keeping me expectant, and when my end is coming (it may be near) I trust: we are expected! We should not understand hope only as our attitude towards others. Others, our mother and father, our children, our friends have set their hope in us. We are their hope, and I believe we humans are also God's hope, and though we are certainly God's disappointment because of what we do or not do to others and to the earth, there is still God's patience with us and deep in our essence there is a divine promise.

You see, you have touched a nerve in my mind and heart. Thank you for your witness of hope. You are no disappointment!

Friede sei mit Dir! my friend,

yours ever,
Jürgen

{Card}   April 2012

Jürgen—

I hope you have a <u>wonderful</u> birthday!

I got your letter. I am <u>beyond excited</u> you are reading and rereading my paper on hope and that I could touch a nerve in your mind and heart!

I am enclosing another paper I wrote on Faith and Hope that I did when we were studying your "Theology of Hope". <u>Enjoy</u>!

Again, <u>happy birthday</u>!

Yours—
Kelly

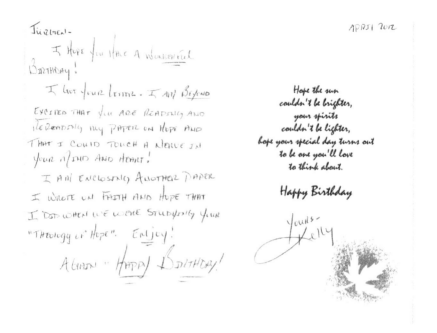

Birthday card from Kelly to Jürgen.

Kelly Gissendaner
Homework
14 Oct. 2011

"Faith and Hope"

In "Theology of Hope" by Jürgen Moltmann on page 20, he states that "faith binds man to Christ. Hope sets this faith open to the comprehensive future of Christ. Hope is therefore the 'inseparable companion' of faith." "Hope is nothing else than the expectation of those things which faith has believed to have been truly promised by God."

Since Sept. 21 I've wondered about Troy Davis's hope and faith leading up to the days he was murdered by the State of Georgia.[154] Then I realized that since that day my hope and faith took a serious nose-dive.

154. Troy Davis's case received national attention because evidence emerged about his likely innocence. See Jen Marlowe and Martina Correia-Davis, *I Am Troy Davis.* Kelly

To me it seems that Moltmann is saying hope and faith go hand-and-hand. That when one dips to the lowest of lows so does the other.

What is faith? Very simply, faith is trust. It is not intellectual acceptance of biblical or theological doctrines, not even the doctrines of Christ or justification. It is confidence in God. Faith is not believing in the Bible. It is not believing in a book, but believing in the God we come to know in the book. Christian faith is not confidence in faith that saves but confidence in the <u>God</u> who saves. This faith is a kind of personal relationship—a total commitment of ourselves to the living God whose trustworthiness has been proved by God's powerful and loving action for us in the life, death and resurrection of Christ.

How can we have such faith? How can we be so sure of God's love that we are freed from the unnecessary, self-defeating attempt to justify ourselves? How can we trust God so completely that we do not have to trust our own goodness or faith? Faith, trust, or assurance in God is a gift. We can no more simply decide to trust God than we can by sheer willpower decide to trust another human being. The faith that trusts in the love of God is itself the work of God's love, revealed to our minds and sealed upon our hearts through the Holy Spirit.

Yet, the fact that we cannot give ourselves faith does not mean that we must say fatalistically that everyone either has or does not have it, that God either does or does not give it, and that there is nothing we can do about it.

Faith does not make us right with God, but no one is made right with God without faith.

Our faith does not force or enable God to love us, but it is our way of acknowledging, receiving, enjoying—and returning—the love that God had for us long before we ever thought of loving God. We are not made right with God <u>by</u> our faith, but we are made right with God <u>through</u> our faith. Our faith does not change God from being against us into being for us, but it does change us from being closed to being open to receive the love God has always had for us.

and Troy exchanged a few letters.

Scripture offers us not one but several hopes for the future. In the writings of the Old Testament for the most part there is no hope at all for life beyond life in the world. Individuals may hope that God will bless the righteous and punish the unrighteous in this life, but after this life there is no heaven and no hell, nor any real life at all. Everyone who dies goes to the same place, Sheol, "the land of gloom and deep darkness" (Job 10:21), a region where all the dead have a kind of shadowy existence completely cut off from God and forgotten by God (Ps 88:4–6, 10–12; 115:17). Israel's hope for the world is not hope for a new heaven and earth that will come at the end of world history but hope for the coming of a new king like David (a "Son of David") who will bring a political kingdom of prosperity, justice, peace and true religion for all people within history. Toward the end of the Old Testament period, Israel's hope for the future changed when the people were carried off into exile. It became clear that in this life it is not the godly who prosper and ungodly who suffer but just the opposite. There was no longer any realistic hope for a Davidic kingdom before which the nations of the earth would bow. There arose an "apocalyptic" hope for a great cosmic battle between God and all the demonic forces of evil at the end of history, at the end of which God will be victorious. At the time all the dead will be raised to "everlasting life" or to "shame and everlasting contempt" (Dan 12:2) to receive the reward or punishment they did not receive in this life, and God (not this or that political leader) will establish an eternal kingdom of righteousness beyond history.

In the New Testament, the book of Revelation develops this apocalyptic hope for the future in greater detail, but it is also the framework for Jesus' own proclamation of the coming of the kingdom of God and for the theology of the New Testament writers. As a result of Jesus' preaching and especially his death and resurrection hope for a final world judgment, the resurrection of the dead and the coming of "a kingdom not of this world" became the foundation of Christian faith. It is important to note, however, that there is no agreement in the New Testament about just when and how all this will happen. Jesus himself seems to have thought that the end of the world and the resurrection of the dead would come soon (Mark 13:30). In his earlier writings, Paul still expects the end to come very soon (1 Thess 4:13-18), but in his later writings (e.g., Romans) he seems to postpone the end to an indefinite future.

I'm not concerned here to trace the details of this development but only to make this one point: we cannot expect to find one neat biblical timetable for the future. Nor can we expect to combine all the relevant texts into one neat scheme describing the way everything will happen. The details of the biblical hope change from time to time and from situation to situation. What we do learn (from the New Testament at least) is that however conflicting and difficult to harmonize are the pictures we are given in different writings, at different points in the development of biblical thinking, they all agree on the basic points: (1) God in Christ stands at the end of history in general; and (2) God in Christ stands at the end of the life of every individual person. That is all we know and all we need to know.

Tübingen, May 14, 2012

Dear Kelly,

"Friede sei mit Dir." How are you? As my medical colleagues told me, Lupus is a serious sickness, a real plague. I can only hope you get a good medical treatment. I am worrying.

Thank you so much for your birthday card that overwhelmed me with a deep feeling of grace. You are very gracious. This year my birthday at 86 fell on Easter Sunday: I sensed the wind of resurrection carrying us through whatever may come.

Thank you also for your trusting me with your "homework" of October 2011 on "Faith and Hope." Your insights in the essence of true human faith are very clear and true. You may however turn also the relationship of God and humans around: It is not only that "in God we trust," God is also trusting in us. God is faithful, so there is also God's faith in us. God believes in you and me whatever disappointments we are making for God. God is waiting for us wherever we have gone lost like the father was trusting and waiting for his son in Luke 15. Your second part on Hope is not so personal as your part on Faith, you are giving too much details of the OT development. Try to meditate on the "God of Hope" (Rom 15:13). His future is not in chronological time but in the time of advent. Therefore there was no real "parousia disappointment" in early Christianity. "The Lord is near" is not a date on the time table, but a life[-]giving existential impression and a personal feeling. For the Hope of Israel see Psalm 42, and then Psalm 73. For the "new heaven and the new earth," read Jesaja [Isaiah] 50, 61 and 65, before you go into Daniel 12. Hope in the OT is transcendent and immanent at the same time. In the NT the Kingdom of God is "not <u>from</u> this world," but <u>in</u> this world. When Jesus said this "not from this world" the kingdom was standing in this world right in front of Pontius Pilate!

Kelly, you are every morning in my mind and prayer.

your brother and friend,
Jürgen

Tübingen, May 14, 2012

Dear Jenny,

Thank you for your long letter of March 4 and for your book and the dear inscription! My correspondence with Kelly is very lively again. She told me about her lupus, sent me a homework of October 2011 on "Faith and Hope" and even congratulated me on my 86 birthday on Easter Sunday this year. My medical friends think lupus is a serious plague. I can only hope Kelly is getting professional treatment in her place. I believe she is so good in "faith seeking understanding" that she should be ordained for prison ministry between her sisters at Arrendale prison. After my visit in that prison I have read more about the American prison system and the mass incarceration of poor people. I am horrified, it looks like the American version of Archipelago Gulag in Soviet-Russia: 600 prisoners of [every] 100,000 people, and in Germany we have 76. And the cheap labor business in prisons. Unbelievable. It is good to care for the prisoners as Murphy and Ed and the beloved Open Door Community are doing, but the whole system must also be changed (from capitalism to democracy).

I hope you are doing fine in the midst of the Iowa cornfields.

With all good wishes,
   your friend,
   Jürgen

July 29, 2012

Jürgen—

How are you? I do apologize for taking so long to respond to your letter. I have been very busy with theology classes and getting ready to teach 2 one hour theology classes on Aug. 10th. I am teaching on exorcism. So, who is Satan? I know according to ancient Christian tradition, he is a creature of God—not a human creature but an angelic creature of some kind. He, and perhaps other angelic creatures with him, rebelled against God and then became the source of the corruption of God's good creation. This understanding of Satan is hinted at in 2 Peter 2:4 and Jude 6, though, in general, Scripture itself shows no interest in where he came from.

So, how shall we modern Christians understand the reality and power of this evil one? Where does evil come from? Can someone <u>really</u> be possessed? These are my questions.

I guess the most common way of explaining the origin of evil is to say that evil comes from the God-given ability all human beings have to choose between good and evil. How could we choose good if evil were not an alternative? Does evil come into our lives and in the world around us because we freely choose evil rather than good?

The answers I have come across and their explanation is neither experientially realistic nor biblical and the answers intensifies rather than solves the problem of the origin of evil. Are we in fact really free to choose either good or evil? I hope you can help me with some answers! ☺

Other than that, I am doing good! I have started cutting grass behind the building I live in and I <u>love</u> the exercise! Plus, I need the exercise!

I'll close this so I can get it on its way. I do pray all is well with you!

Write when you can.

Love your Sister—
Kelly

{Postcard}   September 24, 2012

Dear Kelly,

It is always a pleasure to get a letter from you. Thank you for the one of 29 July. To give you an impression of where I live: this is the Neckar front of our university town. To answer your question: I don't know much of exorcism, at least I have no experience. What I know is that evil spirit can be driven out with the name of Jesus and the sign of the cross. "Evil" spirits are torturing spirits, they have no power over those who are in Jesus Christ. I am glad you can get some exercise. Every morning I pray for the prisoners at Arrendale—and you.

Love and peace,

your brother Jürgen

Tübingen, November 9, 2012

Dear Jenny,

It was most kind of you to send the pictures from the unforgettable prison graduation. Thank you very much. I am grateful for the chance to travel with you to the Arrendale prison and to speak to the graduated students and to talk with Kelly Gissendaner. I was and still am deeply impressed by the situation behind barbed wire. Afterwards I read a lot about the American prison system—and I am still shocked. It is disgusting. All the more I admire the good spirits of the group of prisoners, especially at their graduation.

I am always praying that God may take away the death sentence from Kelly. In your news about the Warden's initiative I see a glimpse of hope. We are corresponding about "exorcism" now. Kelly is having questions about overcoming demonic evil. Can a church ordain Kelly for in-prison-ministry? This would give her a meaning for living in that house.

I am looking forward to your next book on your experiences at the Open Door Community, Atlanta.

Have the courage of hope and the joy of God will be with you.

Love and peace to you,
Jürgen

December 2012

Greetings[155]—

At this Christmas season, I think it's a time to be reminded that God's grace is available to all of us, no matter what sins we have committed. All we have to do is open ourselves up to that grace, to recognize it and be grateful for it.

My message has become one of compassion and hope—a message I am sure would be welcomed by any woman who feels that she has been cast aside and mostly forgotten by the world beyond these prison walls.

I believe each of us was born worthy, that at our core still is a spark of the divine—of the eternal spirit of life—of God; and that we are worthy of love.

---

155. Kelly sent this same Christmas letter to all her friends and family.

I know God loves me as much as He loves Desmond Tutu, even or especially at my most scared and petty and mean and obsessive. <u>LOVES ME; CHOOSES ME</u>!

God is fully loving, and sees us so completely, that God—the Holy Spirit of life and love—continually chooses us all, no matter what mistakes we've made, no matter what others might say about us. We are enough.

Once we entertain the possibility that we don't have to be some idealized version of what it means to be "good," once we understand that who we are at the core of our being is good enough, then we can allow others to be good enough just as they are. We can see the beauty in them, and forgive them.

It doesn't matter who or what we are; it doesn't matter what mistakes we have made in the past; it doesn't matter what size we are, or the color of our skin, or who we love, or whether we are able-bodied, or how much money we have. The world is ours. It's calling us to dream our dreams, to imagine the possibilities that await us, to discover grace and hope.

MERRY CHRISTMAS TO ALL

Love,
Kelly

Jenny, Kelly, and daughter Kayla, Christmas season 2013.

{Postcard}   Tübingen, December 8, 2012

Dear Kelly,

May the "great joy" of Christmas come into your heart and into your cell.
I am praying every morning for you and I hope God hears me. There is a
large network of friends taking care of you. Jenny wrote me a long letter.
She met your daughter. And "The Open Door Community" is a light in
darkness.

    Warm greetings,
    Jürgen

{Facsimile}   Tübingen, January 11, 2013

Dear Jenny,

Warm greetings and all good wishes for the New Year first!

I am somewhat worried because Kelly didn't write or answer my letter. She normally sends a card at Christmas. Did something happen to her? If you know please send me a short Fax.

  In friendship,
  Jürgen

                                               Tübingen, January 20, 2013

Dear Kelly,

Please excuse: I was worried because I hadn't heard from you for a while, so I called Murphy and asked her how you are getting along, and she told me you are fine. I hope that is true—under the circumstance one can't call it "fine." I know because I remember.

Did you take another course in theology or pastoral care? In my imagination you may be a good care-taker and counselor to your sisters in that house.

Give my warm greetings to your daughter. She is really a gift to you, and you may be proud of her.

I am praying every morning that the death sentence may be lifted from you.

  Love and friendship,
  Jürgen

January 21, 2013

Jürgen—

Gut der Morgen.

How are you? I am sorry that it has taken me so long to write. Just know you are not forgotten. You are in my thoughts and heart always.

Before I forget, my lawyer, Susan Casey, will be in Stuttgart in June and would like to travel to Tübingen to meet you while she is there. If you are okay with this meeting you can contact her at . . . Or if you wish she can get your number from Murphy Davis and contact you. Let me know your thoughts on this matter.

My appeal was filed to the 11th Circuit on the 14th day of December. Now we play the waiting game once again.

How was your Weihnachten? Mine was probably one of the better ones I've had in years. I did get to see a lot of family—which was great!

I've just learned that my youngest son is going into the Marines in the summer. I am very proud of him.

And my daughter, whom you met at my theology graduation will probably be engaged soon. I do look forward to grandchildren.

I hope you had a wonderful New Years. I am praying that great things will happen for me in 2013!

I will close this and get it to you. Please let me know about my lawyer visiting with you in June—or you could even let Murphy know and she will let my lawyer know.

If you want you could also check into signing up for my email account and that way we could email one another. Go to jpay.com to find out how to sign up.

Did your new books ever come out? I know when you were here you'd said you had 2 coming out. I would love to get copies of them.

Love in our Christ—
Kelly

April 1, 2013

Jürgen—

How are you? I hope this letter finds you well and very blessed! With this letter I'm also sending along a birthday card for you. I turned 45 on March 8th. I got to spend the day with my daughter. We had an awesome visit!

Dakota, my youngest son, is trying to get into the Marines when he graduates high school in June, which I think will be really good for him.

As for me—I'm doing good. I've been trying to work on losing some weight as that will help with some of my medical issues.

My mind has been on "freedom" a lot. And what that word means.

The Passover story is about freedom. It's a story of how the Israelites went from being slaves in Egypt to being free people with land and a religion of their own. But I wonder when exactly in the story it is that the Hebrew people finally became free.

Does their freedom start when Moses comes to them and says that God has sent him to help them out of bondage? Does it begin when the plagues make them think that Moses might be right, and that God really does want them to be free? Are they free when Pharaoh finally says that they can go? Or is it when they make the choice to actually leave, rushing out of the life they've always known without even taking time to let the bread for the journey rise?

Are they really free when they set out from Egypt, even with Pharaoh's army following after them? Maybe their freedom starts on the edge of the Red Sea, when they look at the water and try to imagine any way that they might get across.

Maybe their freedom came when they actually made it across the sea, and Pharaoh's army did not. That could have been the point at which the Hebrews were really able to imagine themselves as free people, rather than slaves who were running away from their master. Maybe they started to feel free as Miriam sang a song of celebration on the far side of the Red Sea, after they had literally and figuratively crossed over.

But really their journey had only started at this point.

For the next 40 years the Hebrew people wandered in the desert.

I've learned that in Jewish tradition the number forty doesn't really mean an exact number. It's a number that stands for "a really long time." The Hebrew people wander the desert for forty years, and now I understand that it's a whole lot of wandering.

But then the answers to all of my questions hit me that's when freedom happens. Not in a single dramatic moment when Moses lifts up his walking stick and the people follow him across wet sand and flopping fish to a magical world called "freedom." That's not how freedom works. In order to be free you have to escape from the people and systems holding you captive. But once you've done that you still have to get free in your mind! You have to start thinking of yourself as a person who chooses, who has the ability to make things happen in the world, who understands that each of us has both the responsibility and means to shape the world.

That's a huge step, and it doesn't happen overnight. It takes, . . . well, as long as it takes. Often a really long time. And we probably don't even notice any special moment that things changed, but we realize that we are finally a real grown-up supporting ourselves and making our own way in the world.

In the world of the Bible forty years means a really long time, but it doesn't mean forever. Freedom doesn't happen right away, in a single happy moment. But it does happen. Freedom starts when you take the first steps toward a new way of living. And it is complete, well, maybe in something like forty years!

I hope you have a wonderful Birthday! And more to come!

Love in Christ—
Kelly

{Facsimile}   June 3, 2013

Dear Professor Moltmann,

Warm greetings to you, and many thanks for conveying to Murphy Davis your willingness to meet with me and assist in Kelly Gissendaner's legal case. Thank you, too, for all you have done to support Kelly over the past few years. Your friendship has been a source of great strength for her.

As Murphy explained, I will be in Tübingen on Saturday, June 29, and would be grateful to meet with you at 9:30 a.m. if that will work with your schedule. It is my hope that you might be willing to make a brief statement on Kelly's behalf, which I would videotape, that we would use in our efforts to obtain clemency. I would be happy to provide more detailed information about this by phone prior to our meeting.

Please let me know whether a 9:30 meeting on June 29 will work for you, and please also let me know some possible times it would be convenient for me to call you to provide additional information. I very much look forward to talking with you and meeting you.

Kind regards,

Susan C. Casey

Tübingen, June 16, 2013

Dear Ms. Casey,

As promised just a few points for the interview on June 29 at 9:30 in the morning at Tübingen:

1. I know Kelly Gissendaner through a lively exchange of letters since 3 years. It began with Jenny McBride's sending a paper Kelly had written in the theological program on the German theologian Bonhoeffer. I found this very good. During this time Kelly asked for my books in English translation, and our correspondence on theological and spiritual questions became very intensive. She never spoke about her case and I never asked.

2. We met personally at the Graduation Ceremony on Oct. 28, 2011 in the Arrendale Women's Prison. I gave a speech and handed the Certificates to the graduates. Kelly made a personal and very moving speech. Afterwards I was allowed to speak with her and Jenny McBride in a separate room.

3. My impression: Kelly has a strong Christian faith, a warm heart and a sharp mind. It is amazing how she survived more than 12 years on death row. She can say yes to life behind barbed wire, because she found freedom in her soul. I think she is an example many co-prisoners look up to her. She seemed to be like a mother to the young prisoners. She may be a good counselor and a stronghold in the desert of the souls in her place.

   My idea is to give her more education in pastoral care and psychology and appoint her by a church to be a curate among her fellow-prisoners. She has the potential for it, and it would make her life long and meaningful.

Please tell me if you expect more and something different.

Kind regards,

Jürgen Moltmann

{Card}   {No date provided}

Dear Jürgen—

Thank you for doing the interview with my lawyer, Susan Casey. You doing that means more than you know. Susan said she really enjoyed meeting you and talking with you.

As for me,—I'm good. I've been cutting a lot of grass and painting the range I live on. So I've been really busy!

I hope you are well. Forgive me for taking so long to write back.

I am still doing the theology class and I still love it!

Please write when you can and take care of you!

Again—<u>thank you</u> for meeting with my lawyer.

    Love your sister in Christ,
    Kelly

<u>Author's Note</u>: *The prison lost the last batch of letters from Professor Moltmann to Kelly that she had asked to be sent home to her stepmother. Because Professor Moltmann either handwrote or typed his letters on a typewriter, there are no copies of the letters written between the summers of 2013 and 2015.*

{Card}   December 2013

Dear Jürgen—

I have not forgotten you! Never could I do that. This is just a bad season for me because my appeal to the 11th Circuit Court was turned down right before Thanksgiving. I need all the prayers I can get right now because I can't seem to pray for myself.

I'm not in the Christmas Spirit but I am sending out a few cards.

I hope you are doing okay. You hold a very special place in my heart. I hope you have a wonderful Christmas!

> Much love always—
> Kelly

{Card}   December 2014

Jürgen—

Hello my friend! How are you? How is your wife Elisabeth?

I am as good as I can be right now. I am <u>very</u> stressed! I should hear something about an execution date in March. There are 4 guys ahead of me that should get execution dates before me, if the state goes in order. The last execution that happened on the 9th of this month really got to me—to say the least!

The handkerchief that you sent was the <u>most</u> <u>heartfelt</u> thing that I've gotten in my 18 years that I've been locked up. It and the simple note with your words brought tears to my eyes. I am beyond touched! Thank you for your kindness! It means more to me than you know!

I hope you have a <u>wonderful</u> Christmas. Be blessed my friend!

> Love your Sister—
> Kelly

Letters after the Scheduled Execution

April 2, 2015

Dear Jürgen—

I am <u>alive</u>—thank God! God is soooo good!

I finally got the card you sent to me in February. It took forever for me to get it for some reason. But now I have it and thank you so much for the <u>beautiful</u> handkerchief!

I have to pinch myself somedays to make sure I am real and still alive. And of course thanks to God, I am!

I heard there was an article done on you and I there in Germany. I would love to read it! Did you read it? If you did, your thoughts?

I am <u>so</u> thankful to be alive! I can't explain how thankful I am. God is <u>so</u> good!

I have been moved from Arrendale to Pulaski. No one knows why I was moved, but I know no matter where God puts me, God is there also!

I hope you have a wonderful Easter and a very happy birthday. Take care of you and write me when you can.

Love your sis in Christ,

Kelly

July 11, 2015

Dear Jürgen—

I am sorry it has taken me so long to write. As you know things have been crazy!

Thanks be to God—I am still alive and thanking God for each new day that I am alive.

March 2nd was the hardest thing I have ever had to go through. But my faith and hope in God got me through. During the whole thing I refused to let anyone or anything take that faith or hope from me.

I remember on the night at about 10:45 sitting on that bed in that small holding cell and praying, "I will not die but live and declare the works of the Lord!" and repeating over and over "Thank you, Jesus." See I knew one way or another things were about to come to an end, one way or another. 10 minutes later the phone rang and it was one of my attorneys screaming that my execution had been stopped. It was nothing but God! I have often said that God spit in those drugs. Truly I don't know what happened—no one does—but what I do know is that it was nothing but God!

Anyone who doubted there was a God before that should have no doubts anymore!

I hope you are doing good! I am about to start reading your book, "The Way of Jesus Christ." I can't wait to read it!

Please take care of you and write me when you can.

Love your forever sister in Christ—

Kelly

{Card}   August 15, 2015

Dear Jürgen—

It was so good to hear from you. I would love to see you in November—but I've got bad news. The judge dismissed my main appeal which means that I could get an execution date at any time. I'm shocked to say the least!

What I do know when I don't know anything else is that God is in control of all of this. And God showed-up and showed-out twice already and I know God will do it again!

We are all praying at 7:00 p.m. everyday. I hope you will join us. I need all the prayers I can get! Along with my kids and family.

I am still holding out hope that I will see you in November and all of this will be over.

Thank you for all of your support, love, kindness and prayers.

Please write me when you can.

  love in Christ—

  Kelly

{Card}   {No date provided}

Dear Jürgen—

I am looking forward to seeing you in November even though the judge dismissed my appeal. I am still believing in God! God still has control over all of this!

I could get another execution date in September. So keep me in your prayers. We are all praying every day at 7:00 p.m. I'm not sure what time that is there, but your prayers mean a lot to me.

And I am going to keep believing that I will see you in Nov.

  love your sister in Christ!

  Kelly

Dear Kelly,

In these sad days and difficult night my heart and mind are with you, and my thoughts and prayers are with you all the time. Let nobody rob your dignity: you are a beloved daughter of God. Let nobody touch the freedom of your soul: you are a beloved sister of Jesus Christ. Those who want to take your life really don't know what they are doing. Forgive them, their future is dark. You are the truly free one.

On Tuesday, September 29, at 7 PM, I shall lite a candle light and pray for you. You are then not alone. I and thousands of concerned sisters and brothers are with you. You are carried on our prayers and thanksgivings for your life and what you have done in prison over the many years for the imprisoned girls: "mother Kelly." You are an amazing person. I am glad to know you and shall never forget you.

> With compassionate love,
> your friend and brother in Christ,
> Jürgen

October 2, 2015

Dear Children of my friend Kelly,

On Tuesday, September 29, at 9 p.m. our time, I received the sad news "clemency denied" and I was filled with deep sorrow and rage. I lit a candle light and prayed for your mother to thank God for her life and to ask for mercy with her and salvation in the eternal joy. You were included in my prayer.

I am proud and grateful to have learned to know Kelly. Her trust in me and her friendship mean much to me. I remember the first, very formal, letter of hers during a theology-course of Jenny McBride. She had a genuine understanding. "I became so hungry for theology," she said in her unforgettable speech at the graduation day on October 28, 2011 in the Arrendale prison. And she challenged her class: "I implore you not to allow prison to rob you of your dream or vision, not of your dignity or self-worth. Know that suffering can be redeemed. Through Divine grace our life is not wasted. Let us put off hatred and envy and put on love and compassion—every day!" And she did this until her last day. She lived and died in this strong faith. On Friday last week I sent her my last letter, and she answered: "I am strong." I admire her so much. In my younger years I spent 3 years in a prisoner-of-war camp, and Kelly suffered 18 years on a death-row! Her faith grew stronger and stronger. This was like a miracle. I myself found consolation in her letters and cards, so full of love. Once she sent me a self-made drawing of a little village with big trees and a small church. Did you know she was drawing so beautifully?

I shall treasure her letters and shall never forget such an amazing person as Kelly was. May the God of all consolation bless you with peace and strengthen you in your love for life and the courage to be.

With love and com-passion,

Yours ever,

Jürgen

Jürgen Moltmann

Part 3

The Dawning of a New Day

THE THEOLOGICAL NARRATIVE IN Part 1 ends with a concern addressed to Professor Moltmann: How are we to understand hope in light of Kelly's execution? It is a crucial question since the end of Kelly's story is, as one reader put it, "devastating"—for those who lived it and even for those who read about it now. Naming the devastation is one way we witness to its horror. It is an appropriate response to the reality that occurred.

At the same time, the devastation we feel is potentially debilitating. It can work on us, stripping our energy and determination to fight against the very thing we denounce. While I have told Kelly's story repeatedly in a variety of settings since her execution, to honor her memory and with an aim toward abolition, it is also true that it has been hard for me at times to even do small acts of advocacy because of my latent sense of despair. Moltmann's theology of hope requires that we identify this tendency toward despair and fight the temptation to give into it, but without masking the horror. His answer—"hope is protest"—includes and takes seriously our reason for despair, because central to the work of hope is fighting against the powers that caused the devastation.

Hope as protest no doubt described our advocacy work *before* Kelly's execution. We were protesting the Parole Board's devastating denial of clemency. We understood hope in the way that Moltmann taught us—as living in the tension between false certainties, be it the certainty of despair, on the one hand, or shallow optimism on the other, often expressed through Christian platitudes about God. Both of these certainties tempt passivity, either the belief that nothing we do will matter or the belief that God won't let something happen that isn't meant to be, so we need not get involved. Instead, biblical hope calls Christians to obey Jesus' commands and live into the kingdom of God now, which requires that we fight death-dealing powers and present injustice that counter God's reign. As we took up this fight during the advocacy campaign, many of us experienced energy and courage born from hope that we didn't know we had. I had never experienced the power of God's Spirit as intensely as I did during our campaign. It is also true that I had never been so close to the powers and principalities of death as I was while accompanying Kelly, and as a result of seeing them up close, I have never believed so strongly in the God of life and liberation. As I have told Kelly's story to groups around the country, I have mustered the energy to do so by holding tight to these experiences that reveal truths I cannot deny.

Even so, for many of us, a crippling devastation remains years after Kelly's execution. In the words of two disciples on their walk to Emmaus, I hear echoes of my own lament: "*We had hoped*" (Luke 24:21). "Jesus' helpless death on the cross is the end of [the disciples'] hope," writes Moltmann, and to a certain extent, Kelly's helpless execution ended mine.[1] The antidote to our devastation, I've come to see, is to find a way to hope after hope—in the words of 1 Peter, to be "*born again* to a *living hope*" (1:3).

The kind of hope Moltmann writes about—1 Peter's living hope—is rarely practiced by Christians, in large part because the dominant theological traditions we have inherited have ignored its biblical foundation. This is exactly why Moltmann wrote his *Theologie der Hoffnung* in 1964: "to give back to Christianity its authentic hope for the world."[2] It is this theology that enraptured Kelly and gave her a new love for life even on death row. And, so, it is only fitting that it is to Moltmann's theology we turn as we seek to build from the ruins of Kelly's execution and be born again to a living hope. This hope, 1 Peter tells us, is rooted in "the resurrection of Jesus Christ from the dead" (1:3). It is a *living* hope with this-worldly consequence.

But before we turn to Moltmann's theology of hope, we need to clear the ground by examining how our prior theological formation may hinder our growth in this-worldly hope. Specifically, we need to examine what we have been taught about the crucifixion of Jesus. Kelly's story prompts this investigation, not only because it includes her own execution but also because contested notions about Jesus' cross found their way into her clemency hearing with deleterious effect. A theology of hope that grapples with

1. Moltmann, *Sun of Righteousness*, 44.
2. Moltmann, *Broad Place*, 101.

Kelly's execution must grapple with Jesus' own. Simply put, a theology of this-worldly hope cannot find a home in the theological framework most of us have been given. The good news is there is a way to understand the cross that makes better sense of the biblical witness and stirs us toward a living hope.

Contesting Crucifixion

In the Introduction, I refer to the account of Kelly's faith and our advocacy as a theological narrative, a story with theological significance that is most readily seen when placing it within the larger story the Bible tells—one about restoration and forgiveness, the possibility and promise of transformed life, and the call to struggle against the powers and principalities of death. Reading Kelly's story through a biblical lens enabled us to tell a more truthful story about her and about the death penalty than the criminal legal system allows. It is equally true that her story, culminating in her execution, has helped me better understand the biblical texts, especially the crucifixion of Jesus, in a visceral way that also has theological implications. Experiencing the horror of Kelly's execution—and the role of God's Spirit in empowering our resistance to it—has helped me better understand the horror of Jesus' crucifixion and the crucifixion as an event that counters God's intended reign.

Execution in all its forms is a traumatic event that harms everyone in its reach. This reality compels us to reconsider how we speak of Jesus' crucifixion and God's role in it. As we saw in Kelly's story, the way Christians understand the meaning of the cross has ethical implications, sometimes as serious as life and death. Underscoring the link between ethics and theology, Jesus says in the Sermon on the Mount that every good tree bears good fruit and every bad tree bears bad fruit (Matt 7:15–20). We can trust the truthfulness of our theological convictions when they bear good fruit, and we must reconsider our theological convictions when they bear bad fruit. The Parole Board held a particular theology of the cross and had the power to implement it. They claimed that Jesus' crucifixion validated Kelly's execution because it showed that "good can come from death." They argued that God is okay with crucifixion because Jesus didn't use divine power to get himself or the thief off the cross. And the fruit their theology bore was Kelly's execution.[3]

---

3. While the actions of the Board cannot be reduced to their theological convictions

The Parole Board's theological claims don't come out of nowhere. They arise out of popular understandings of the meaning of the cross, especially among privileged Western Christians, which must be examined and replaced with an interpretation that is at once more faithful to the biblical witness and that honors the lived experiences of people suffering contemporary crucifixions in every form.

Like the Board of Pardons and Paroles, most Christians today understand the theological significance of the cross through a popularized mixture of the "theory of satisfaction" and the "substitutionary atonement theory." The satisfaction theory was first articulated by the medieval theologian Anselm in the eleventh century, later developed into a theory based on penal substitution by Reformed thinkers like John Calvin in the sixteenth century, and is now the dominant understanding of the meaning of the cross among the majority of North American Christians. Anselm's atonement theory arose out of his medieval context of feudal lords and their serfs and the medieval culture's understanding of law and order, in which a serf's disobedience dishonors the feudal lord. Later theologians came to think of sin's offense less in terms of honor and more in terms of wrath. Because a serf's disobedience dishonors the feudal lord, satisfaction must be paid or there will be punishment. In the same way, the theory goes, human disobedience dishonors God and so satisfaction must be paid or punishment will follow. Because sinful humanity cannot make satisfaction, God becomes a human being and pays the price on our behalf. God satisfies the debt owed to God. Or in penal substitutionary terms, although sinful human beings deserve the punishment of death, God in Christ vicariously suffers the punishment demanded by God in our place.

Most Christians are familiar with this theory of atonement, known best through its popular formulation, "Jesus died for my sins." For many Christians, this theory constitutes the core of Christian faith, so much so that reconsidering it would feel like giving up the faith. What will become clear, I hope, is that re-examining the role that Jesus' death plays in salvation leads us not away from the good news of the gospel or the biblical witness but more deeply into it. The good news is that there is a better gospel than what many of us have been given, one that sounds and feels like truly good

---

alone (since our religious, political, and cultural formation influence and reinforce one another), theology often serves as a weighty authority that legitimates ideas we already have. Therefore, it must be examined, especially when those convictions legitimate dehumanization and death. The aim is *metanoia*, the renewal of our minds that enables a changed course of action leading to transformed social practices (Rom 12:2).

news. We have already heard its melodies in Parts 1 and 2, for example, in the theological conversations between Professor Moltmann and Kelly and in some of Kelly's own theological reflections. This gospel energizes love for this life and the life of every human being and broadens our attention from the cross to the incarnation and resurrection—to a new world born in the midst of the old, based on God's reign.

The fundamental problem with the satisfaction or substitutionary atonement theory is that it confines the moment of salvation to the crucifixion, rather than interpreting the meaning of Jesus' death through the incarnation and resurrection. Many twentieth and twenty-first century theologians and biblical scholars have come to see that the Apostle Paul understood the whole Christ event—the incarnation, crucifixion, and resurrection—to be salvific. In doing so, they return to the views held by Christians in the first thousand years, who centered their faith (and art) on the incarnation and resurrection.[4] When Christians understand Jesus' salvific work through the entire Christ event, we are able to align Paul's theology in the epistles with Jesus' life and ministry as recorded in the Gospel narratives.

The satisfaction or substitutionary theory can be articulated and understood without any reference to the Gospel narratives. All one needs to accept is the formula that Jesus died on the cross for our sins. Jesus then functions as more of "an idea-principle in a theological system" than a historical person, the Word become flesh. As theologian James Cone says, "We cannot have a human Jesus unless we have a historical Jesus, that is, unless we *know* his history. That is why the writers of the four Gospels tell the good news in the form of the story of Jesus' life."[5] When Christians start to take seriously the historical life and ministry of Jesus and the historical details depicted in the Gospels, the satisfaction/substitutionary account does not hold up.

Because faithfulness to the New Testament witness demands that Christians hold together the Pauline epistles and the Gospel narratives, Mennonite biblical scholar and theologian J. Denny Weaver has coined the term "Narrative Christus Victor" to describe Christ's work of salvation. "Narrative" refers to the Gospel accounts of Jesus' life, death, and resurrection, while "Christus Victor" refers to Paul's view that what Jesus engaged

---

4. Weaver, *Nonviolent Atonement*, 109, citing Brock and Parker, *Saving Paradise*, ix, 223.

5. Cone, *God of the Oppressed*, 109.

in and won was a cosmic battle between the reign of God and the forces of evil and death that oppose God's earthy reign. This is the heart of Paul's theology, what biblical and theological scholars call "Paul's apocalyptic theology." "Apocalypse" in Greek means "revelation," the unveiling of what was previously unknown, and so Paul's apocalyptic theology is his understanding of what God was revealing in the life, death, and resurrection of Jesus, what God accomplished through his person and work. What God revealed not only has cosmic significance but also ethical implications for social and political life. For, as the language already conveys, the "reign" or "kingdom" of God is inherently political: it concerns how human beings order our lives together. Paul's apocalyptic theology fueled the communal life and public witness of the early Christians. And it is a helpful and important lens for contemporary Christians who wish to live in a way that challenges and offers an alternative to the forces of evil and death that shape our society today.

We might summarize the Narrative Christus Victor understanding of salvation this way: Through the Christ event—through the life, death, and resurrection of Jesus of Nazareth—God proclaims an interconnected, "Yes-No-Yes." In the incarnation, God proclaims "Yes!" as Jesus embodies the reign of God on earth. In the crucifixion, God proclaims "No!" to the powers and principalities of evil and death that oppose God's reign and kill Jesus. And in the resurrection, God proclaims "Yes!" to the cosmic victory of God's reign, the triumph over the powers and principalities, and the start of a new world.

Reducing the salvific event to the crucifixion amounts to locating God's intent in the "No" part of the proclamation, in the things that God has opposed and judged. In the crucifixion, God says "No!" to retributive punishment, violence, and death. But the satisfaction/substitutionary theory takes the very things God has condemned and makes them necessary ingredients for salvation. In this theory, God's justice is not fundamentally restorative but retributive, and violence is redemptive.[6] In the formula "Jesus died for my sins," we hear murmurs of grace and good news since God has indeed done something "for us" (Gal 2:20; 3:13). And from the cross we undoubtedly hear Jesus speak words of forgiveness to those who are putting

6. Western Christians have tended to understand God's justice as retributive. "Retribution" means giving back to someone what they deserve or repayment for what one has done, either through reward or punishment. Understood as retribution, God's justice is seen narrowly through a forensic frame, has a negative connotation, and is characterized by punishment and vengeance.

him to death: "Father forgive them, for they don't know what they are do-ing" (Luke 23:34). But when the forgiveness of individual sin or salvation depends on punishment, retribution, and violence (even when the one who pays the price is God in Jesus Christ), Christians become confused about what is good and what is evil. Like the Parole Board members who said of Kelly's execution that "good can come from death," we become people who call evil "good," instead of calling the thing what it is: trauma and harm, state-sanctioned murder, the condemnation of a child of God. The sad result is that Christians become supporters of evil deeds and agents of the powers of death that contradict God's reign. Christian confusion over good and evil shows up in a range of political commitments, most readily seen in how comfortable many of us are with laws, policies, customs, and attitudes that condemn human beings. While attempting to be faithful to God, tragically, we confuse God's Yes with God's No. The good news is that the crucifixion *is* God's "No!" to condemnation, retribution, and violence. The good news is that God's "Yes!" encompasses more than most of us pre-viously imagined (Eph 3:20).

God's "Yes!" in Christ first takes shape through the incarnation itself. As the Word become flesh, Jesus embodies the kingdom of God on earth. The Gospel narratives describe Jesus' mission as "making visible the reign of God" in history, a reign that is in conflict with the powers and forces of evil and death.[7] Through Jesus, the reign of God confronts oppression and injustice and counters the powers and principalities that enslave our world and damage relationships among human beings. "The Spirit of the Lord is upon me," Jesus says in his first public address, "because I have been chosen to bring good news to the poor. God has sent me to proclaim liberty to the captives and recovery of sight to the blind, to set free the oppressed and announce that the time has come when the Lord will save the people" (Luke 4:18–19). As Jesus makes clear, the reign of God is good news for those whom society has cast out and condemned. For his mission is to set people free by delivering them from any communal structure or societal force that holds them captive and causes them harm. The good news of the incarna-tion is that the kingdom of God has already taken root in history through the life and ministry of Jesus. As the embodiment of the kingdom of God, Jesus' public ministry poses an alternative to the powers of this world, as it struggles nonviolently against them.

---

7. Weaver, *Nonviolent Atonement*, 40–46.

Because of the incarnation, we know what the reign of God looks like. It is made manifest by specific practices revealed in the ministry of Jesus and articulated through his Gospel commands. These commands include: love your neighbor (Mark 12:31); do not condemn other human beings (Luke 6:37); do not judge the moral status or worth of others (Matt 7:1); do not resist evil with evil (Matt 5:39); confront oppressive structures with nonviolent creative action (Matt 5:38–42);[8] put up the sword (Matt 26:52); cast out demons and oppressive principalities; heal and restore (Matt 10:8); make restitution and repair harm (Luke 19:1–10); love your enemies (Matt 5:44); forgive others (Matt 6:12–15); have mercy (Matt 5:7); make peace (Matt 5:9); welcome strangers, visit the prisoner, care for the sick, feed the hungry (Matt 25:35–36); repent and bear fruit worthy of God's kingdom (Matt 4:17; 3:2–8); and do my commandments (Luke 6:46). Because the commandments of Jesus are practices that make God's kingdom visible and concrete, they are practices that have social and political implications. When Christians obey Jesus' commands, we participate in God's intended social order, in God's kingdom come. Like the first disciples who followed after Jesus, we are invited to join his work, here and now. We are invited into a range of practices that foster abundant life and conform to the ministry of the incarnate God.

If, in the satisfaction or substitutionary atonement theory, the life of Jesus has no functional role in the work of salvation—Jesus was, in essence, born to die—in the Gospels the opposite is true. The life of Jesus and the coming of God's kingdom are definitively interconnected. Already in the Gospel narratives, as a result of the incarnation and before the crucifixion, the gospel of Jesus Christ is revealed. The gospel is, as Jesus himself says, "the good news of the kingdom of God" (Luke 4:43). The good news includes but is more than God's forgiveness of my individual sin. The good news is that Jesus has inaugurated the reign of God on earth, and we are invited to follow him and participate in it. In the Synoptic Gospels, references to Jesus, the gospel, and the kingdom of God are interchangeable, so much so that we cannot separate the person of Jesus from his commands, which show us how to make visible God's earthly reign.[9] When John the

8. See Wink, *Jesus and Nonviolence*, chapter 2.

9. For example, similar texts in Mark 10:29, Matthew 19:29, and Luke 18:29 interchange Jesus, the kingdom, and the good news. As Philip Ziegler argues, this strong link between Jesus and the kingdom is found in early church fathers like Tertullian, who writes that the gospel concerns "the Kingdom of God, Christ himself," and in Origen's writings, who coins the term *autobasileia*, meaning "the kingdom in person" (*Militant*

Baptist sees Jesus coming to the river Jordan to be baptized, for example, he proclaims, "Look, the kingdom of God has drawn near!" So strong is this link between Jesus and the kingdom that Christians cannot claim to know, trust, or be faithful to Jesus if we ignore his teachings or reject the practices that constitute his reign (Luke 6:46). We cannot hear Jesus' command, "do not condemn," and then support execution. We must guard against defining faithfulness to Jesus in the public realm in ways that counter his straightforward commands.

Jesus' mission was to make visible the reign of God on earth and he remained faithful to that mission even as it led to his own crucifixion. His ministry and teachings—good news for the poor, oppressed, and condemned—brought him into direct conflict with imperial Rome and its local political and religious leaders. With the support of the masses, these rulers condemned Jesus and put him to death. In doing so, they served as agents of the powers and principalities that Paul refers to in his letters. While Paul's terminology is not of his making (it was present in Jewish apocalyptic writings), he infuses the language of powers with new meaning. Instead of assigning them a purely spiritual referent, Paul defines powers and principalities as "structures of earthly existence" that are in bondage to evil and in a fallen world create conditions of domination.[10] These powers include any societal institution or economic order, any legal system or framework of morality, any religious belief or political ideology, any cultural norm or attitude—any order or force larger than us that shapes our lives and has formative influence over our thinking and behavior but is antithetical to the reign of God.

Jesus was killed by the political and religious establishment because of the life he chose to live in solidarity with the outcast and condemned, in resistance to the prevailing social order. His death was nothing short of the "rejection of the rule of God" by powers and principalities that oppose that rule.[11] As the Gospels make clear, the actor(s) responsible for Jesus' death was not a God that demands punishment but the forces opposed to God's reign. Jesus willingly, obediently, lovingly, and sacrificially fulfilled his mission of witnessing to God's earthly reign, even unto death. That death is rightly understood only if we take into consideration what came

---

Grace, 85).

10. Berkhof, *Christ and the Powers*, 16–19, 23–24.

11. Weaver, *Nonviolent Atonement*, 47.

before—Jesus' particular mission and ministry that threatened the social order and the powers that be.

It is equally true that Jesus' crucifixion plays a salvific role only in light of what follows—his resurrection from the dead. The cross is a momentary—but, nevertheless, existentially real—triumph of the powers and principalities over Jesus. The experience of being crushed by the powers of condemnation and death is tantamount to being godforsaken, as evidenced in Jesus' words from the cross, "My God, my God why have you forsaken me?" (Matt 27:46). The resurrection, in turn, is the cosmic victory of God's reign over the powers. It is the condemnation of condemnation. Jesus' crucifixion exposes the powers and judges them for what they are—forces that counter God's reign. In light of the resurrection, Paul can claim that on the cross Jesus "disarmed the rulers and authorities and made a public example of them, triumphing over them" (Col 2:15). Jesus disarms the powers and principalities through his commitment to nonviolence, his willingness to endure suffering for the sake of others rather than continue the cycle of harm. As contemporary practitioners of nonviolent resistance know well, by absorbing in his own body the forces of violence and domination, Jesus interrupts the cycle of evil and stops its momentum, in turn, "making peace through his blood on the cross" (Col 1:20). There Jesus unmasks the powers of evil and death and reveals crucifixion for what it is—injustice masquerading as justice, evil masquerading as a social good.

For Paul, the cross is judgment on the old age ruled by powers of evil and death, and the resurrection announces a new age ruled by the power of God. The resurrection is both the "victory over evil and death in the old order and also the beginning of the transformation of fallen creation in the new order."[12] In light of the resurrection, the cross for Paul is the axis or hinge upon which the ages turn.[13] This is why he speaks so often of it. As the dawn of a new age, the resurrection also points back to the incarnation, namely, to the practices that constitute God's reign. Through the resurrection, God validates Jesus' life and ministry and shows that Jesus' commands are realistic prescriptions for overcoming evil in this world.

For Paul, God's victory is sure. In the "fullness of time," God will "gather up" and restore "all things" (Eph 1:20), for he has already "reconciled all things" to himself (Col 1:20). Even so, the new age of God's reign

12. Weaver, *Nonviolent Atonement*, 52. See also Beker, *Paul the Apostle*, chapter 8.

13. Ziegler, *Militant Grace*, 159. See also Martyn, *Theological Issues in the Letters of Paul*, 93–94.

and the old age ruled by evil and death overlap in time in our present world. There is no easy transition between the passing away of the old age and the onset of the new, only a continued struggle between competing powers. As limited yet responsible human beings, we are at once passive victims and complicit agents vulnerable to the powers. We wake up in the middle of things, inheriting a society and situations not of our making, and we readily become formed by forces larger than ourselves—"actively habituated" to their ways.[14] We become complicit with, even instruments of, destructive forces that do us harm and harm others whom we are called to love.

Sin is the name for our bondage to these powers, and so salvation requires deliverance. When Jesus triumphed over the powers of evil and death, he opened the way of salvation through the power of the resurrection, delivering human beings from bondage and inviting us to participate in the power of the Spirit of God instead. Since the good news is the present reality and possibility of God's reign, salvation is best understood as an "invitation" to "begin to be free" from the powers of evil and death by living a life "shaped and marked by the story of Jesus."[15] This is why Jesus teaches his disciples to pray, "deliver us from evil" and "your kingdom come . . . on earth" (Matt 6:9–13). Living this life requires acknowledging the ways that we—even as Christians seeking to be faithful to God—have been complicit in maintaining the powers of condemnation and death, be it as active agents or blind adherents. We acknowledge our enslavement to particular powers and then actively repent by living a life that submits to the rule of God by obeying Jesus' commands. Salvation includes freedom *from* powers that enslave and freedom *for* the kingdom of God.

More and more, I've come to see that Paul's understanding of sin as bondage to powers larger than ourselves is absolutely essential for personal and social transformation. I find Paul's language of powers and principalities helpful for naming and responding to evil and injustice, especially in light of his letter to the Ephesians, where he writes, "For our struggle is not against flesh and blood but against the rulers, against the authorities, against the cosmic powers of this present darkness" (6:12). The fight, in other words, is not against other human beings but against the powers that enslave us all. This is why Jesus directs his condemnation to the powers, not ordinary human beings; for, what people need is not condemnation but deliverance (John 3:17). This is a truth that Martin Luther King Jr. embodied

14. Ziegler, *Militant Grace*, 62.

15. Weaver, *Nonviolent Atonement*, 46–47.

and proclaimed throughout the civil rights movement as he spoke of "the struggle to defeat the forces of evil" and of "a revolution against injustice, not against fellow citizens."[16] As Dr. King showed so well while adopting this Pauline framework, we're all in this together. A Pauline understanding of the powers guards against a moral dualism that separates and essentializes people as good or evil. Instead, it equalizes as it identifies that we all need deliverance. We all need deliverance from the various powers that control and distort our lives, and we all need healing from their harmful effects. And yet, liberation and healing will look different depending on one's relationship to the particular power. Those who are complicit in maintaining destructive powers must be liberated from known and unknown participation in them, which distorts our personality and relationship with others, and those who are oppressed or crushed by the powers need to be released from their suffering and given resources for restoration and healing.

What this means is that salvation requires deliverance from multiple angles. At times we are instruments of destructive powers that harm other human beings (whether as active agents or passive adherents), and at times we are oppressed by the powers, suffering underneath them. Kelly and Professor Moltmann's stories both testify to this. Kelly acted as an agent of death-dealing powers when she planned the murder of her husband Doug, and she became a victim crushed by the power of death as she suffered execution. Professor Moltmann was enlisted as an agent of the powers of death as a youth conscripted into the German army, simultaneously becoming a victim of powers larger than himself and an instrument of the Nazi regime, and he suffered under the powers and principalities as a prisoner of war. In each of their stories we see places where the Spirit of God was working for their deliverance and making it concrete: For Kelly, in the faithfulness of pastoral counselors who helped her face what she had done, in her children's forgiveness and their reconciliation, in opportunities for creative ministry to others, in theological education and the community formed around it, in friendship inside and outside prison walls, in a loving and dedicated legal team, in threats of snow and cloudy drugs, and in an international advocacy movement that arose on her behalf, up until her execution which was, like Jesus' own, a momentary but existentially

---

16. King Jr., *Strength to Love*, 83. See also Harding, *Inconvenient Hero*, 18. Paul's language of powers and principalities is a helpful framework for personal transformation because it invites reflection beyond common notions of morality, which tend to be highly individualistic, and instead points toward our complicity in social structures and systems that do harm.

real triumph of the powers and principalities, one that reverberates today. For Moltmann, we see the Spirit's work of deliverance in the defeat of the Nazi regime, in the hospitality shown by Scottish families as a prisoner of war, in the reading of Scripture and growing awareness that the "assailed, forsaken Christ" understood him completely and was "a companion on the way," in theological education and ministry training, in reconciliation with a group of Dutch Christians, in release from prison, and in his abundant life thereafter, characterized by groundbreaking theological reflection and friendships across the globe. These manifestations of deliverance are the result of both divine and human action—the movement of God and the movement of communities empowered by the Spirit of God to resist powers and principalities that condemn.

Paul's apocalyptic theology encompasses not only what God has already done in Christ but also what God promises still to do through the power of the Spirit. Already accomplished is the nonviolent triumph of the reign of God over the powers of evil and death and the beginning of a new world. What is promised is the restoration of all things—a new earth—the eschatological reign in which the last enemy, death, will exist no more (1 Cor 15:25, Rev 21:1). We may understand the reign of God, then, through the phrase, "even now, only then completely."[17] The call of the Christian is to participate in the reign of God even now, through the power of the Spirit, who is for us today "the present power" of God's reign.[18] This is what it means to be "in Christ," namely, to live into the new age. For, as Paul says, "If anyone is in Christ, there is a new creation. Everything old has passed away; see, everything has become new!" (2 Cor 5:17). The good news Paul proclaims is this: God has inaugurated a new age and human communities may conform to it. God has done a new thing and we are empowered to live it out![19]

Living Hope

Moltmann's theology of hope aligns with the Narrative Christus Victor or Pauline Apocalyptic framework sketched above. No one, in my estimation, has written more movingly or shown more clearly the implications of this framework for our lives. Moltmann's theology of hope has the power to

17. Ziegler, *Militant Grace*, 104–5.

18. Ziegler, *Militant Grace*, 72.

19. Ziegler, *Militant Grace*, 173, citing Martyn, *Galatians*, 103.

shape our theological imaginations and inform our habits, influencing our patterns of thinking and moving us toward creative action in the world. In this last section, I examine components of his theology that not only have reminded me of my conversion to hope years ago in graduate school but also have sparked new life in me now, after the death of hope, and initiated the process of being born again to a living hope. These aspects of hope have the capacity to inspire resistance to the death penalty and related powers, confidence that such work is not in vain, and love for a God who loves this earth and our lives in it. This hope, Moltmann says as he echoes Paul's gospel, positions us "at the dawn of a new day at the point where night and day, things passing and things to come, grapple with each other."[20] Hope gives us courage to live in this moment as we proclaim with our lives that a new world is dawning.

The first thing to be said about a theology of hope is that it is the essential core of Christian life and witness. It's what it's all about. Hope is not "one element *of* Christianity" or an "epilogue" to Christian faith but "the key in which everything . . . is set." It is the "glow" that radiates from "the dawn of an expected new day." In the introduction to *Theology of Hope*, Moltmann explains that eschatology, the doctrine that encompasses the objects of Christian hope—the promises of God—has misleadingly been called the doctrine of the last things. In "relegating" events like the return of Christ, the restoration of the world, the coming of the kingdom, the resurrection of the body, and the new creation of all things to the "last day," Christians rob them of their "directive, uplifting and critical significance for all the days which are spent here . . . in history." Eschatology is best understood as the doctrine of Christian hope, which embraces both the promises of God and the this-worldly, hope-filled action inspired by those promises. A theology of hope includes the promises proclaimed in the Old and New Testaments, promises that carry immediacy within them. "I am about to do a new thing," God declares through the prophet Isaiah; "now it springs forth, do you not perceive it? I will make a way in the wilderness and rivers in the desert" (Isa 43:19). Paul refers to this God as "the God of hope" (Rom 15:13), the God of the Bible who "calls into existence the things that do not exist" (Rom 4:17) and who "makes all things new" (Rev 21:5; cf. 2 Cor 5:17). Christians anticipate the nearness of the fulfillment of God's promises by living into them today. When we do so we exhibit a hope

20. Moltmann, *Theology of Hope*, 31.

that is "forward looking and forward moving" while also "revolutionizing and transforming the present."[21]

Second, a theology of hope is rooted in the resurrection of Jesus Christ from the dead. Christian hope *is* hope in the resurrection.[22] From the beginning, for Paul and the early Christians, the resurrection was "*the* primal fact" of their faith and the foundation of their confession that Jesus is Lord (Rom 10:8–9).[23] "If Christ has not been raised, then our proclamation has been in vain, and your faith has been in vain," Paul writes to the church in Corinth (1 Cor 15:14).

Through the resurrection, the power of death and sin has been broken. "Death has been swallowed up in victory," Paul writes to the Corinthians. "Thanks be to God, who gives us the victory through our Lord Jesus Christ" (15:54–56). "With these unforgettable words Paul celebrates the victory of life over death and sin, which make a hell out of life in this world," writes Moltmann. And yet, he continues, "we do not find it so easy to bring ourselves to utter this song of liberty." Against the backdrop of a history of human suffering, the power of death feels unbroken in our lives here on earth and Easter seems absurd. Instead, "victory seems swallowed up in death, and hell triumphs . . . here and now," he writes. "But things are quite different if, like Paul and the first Easter witnesses, we learn to see the everyday history of suffering in the perspective of Christ's resurrection."[24] Here Moltmann does not mean that the resurrection serves as an otherworldly consolation *after* suffering and death. Rather, the resurrection announces that another world is possible. "The purification of the earth from 'sin and death' already begins now."[25] In light of this conviction, "it begins to be absurd to see violence and death as a matter of course. Nothing is inevitable. Nothing has to be put up with."[26] With the raising of Jesus, "the last days have already begun. These are the final days of this world of sin, violence and death, and at the same time they are the first days of the new world of righteousness and justice, peace and eternal life (Rom 13:12)." Jesus' resurrection is the beginning of the new creation of all things, for he is, according to Paul, "the first born from the dead" and "the first born of all

21. All quotes in paragraph from Moltmann, *Theology of Hope*, 15–16.

22. Moltmann, *Theology of Hope*, 18.

23. Moltmann, *Sun of Righteousness*, 39, 45.

24. Moltmann, *Power of the Powerless*, 122–23.

25. Moltmann, *Sun of Righteousness*, 81.

26. Moltmann, *Power of the Powerless*, 123.

creation" (Col 1:15, 18). Easter marks the first day of the new creation, the beginning of the cosmic transformation "of this transitory world into its true and abiding form."[27]

A theology of hope proclaims, then, that "God's future has already begun" in the resurrection of Jesus Christ from the dead.[28] God's future is best understood (as Moltmann writes in a letter to Kelly) in terms of advent, not chronological time. The future is "what is coming to meet us."[29] This is why he says in *Theology of Hope* that "Christian eschatology speaks of Jesus Christ and *his* future. It recognizes the reality of the raising of Jesus and proclaims the future of the risen Lord."[30] Christian hope is directed toward the future that God brings—the kingdom of God on earth and the new creation of all things. Christians who live this hope actively ready themselves for God's immanent coming by preparing the way through repentance made concrete in creative and courageous obedience to Jesus' commands. "Prepare the way of the Lord," Isaiah proclaims and John the Baptist echoes, "make straight in the desert a highway for our God" (Isa 40:3, Mark 1:3). As John the Baptist makes clear, this preparation embraces our social and political lives since it is preparation for the kingdom of God (Matt 3:2). By preparing the way, human beings do not initiate God's coming but rather respond to the promise and, in doing so, participate in the new world God brings. Preparing the way in hope means "trusting in God's promise, seeing the world in the advance radiance of God's future, and living life here as a foretaste of God's fullness."[31]

Because God's future has already begun in the risen Jesus and meets us in the present—inaugurating the new creation of all things—the resurrection gives Christians a new perspective on the world. The state of the world is not best understood as fallen but transforming. Christian positions on social and political issues are often rooted in a conviction that the world is fallen and that institutions like the death penalty are necessary fixtures of society given human sin. These views are easier to hold when we are not the ones directly impacted by their harm or when we remain distant from people like Kelly who are. If the world is presumed to be fixed in its fallen

27. Moltmann, *Sun of Righteousness*, 46, 68.

28. Moltmann, *In the End—the Beginning*, 48.

29. Moltmann, *Jesus Christ for Today's World*, 140. See also Moltmann, *Coming of God*, 22–29.

30. Moltmann, *Theology of Hope*, 17.

31. Moltmann, *Sun of Righteousness*, 184.

form, then institutions of control like our prison system and tools of domination like capital punishment are seen as realistic ways to address and
manage sin. We already know empirically that this is not the case. Capital
punishment and mass incarceration do not decrease violence or heal harms
but manufacture violence and harm.[32]

An imagination shaped by a theology of hope is not beholden to the
logic of a fallen world, which operates as if the world is fixed and denies
the transformative power of the resurrection. Rather, "hope alone is to be
called 'realistic,'" Moltmann argues, "because it alone takes seriously the
possibilities with which all reality is fraught." Everything that God has
promised is "within the bounds of possibility."[33] The "knowledge that there
can be change" establishes the "reasonableness of hope."[34] And so, belief
in the resurrection means belief in possibility—the possibility of a fundamental change in the present state of things, not only for us personally but
also as a society. Christians demonstrate this hope through "passion for the
possible," specifically, "a passion for what has been made possible" through
the risen Christ. To believe in the resurrection means "to cross in hope
and anticipation the bounds that have been penetrated by the raising of the
crucified."[35] God's promise "throws open the future."[36]

"God promises the new creation of all things," Moltmann observes,
"but human beings behave as if everything remains as it was."[37] Because
dominant Christian traditions have not emphasized the present power of
the resurrection, Christians tend to think that belief in it simply means
"considering Christ's resurrection to be true and hoping for a life after
death." The resurrection is seen as historical fact but without meaningful
consequence for historical lives, only a statement of faith or perhaps a point
of apologetics to be defended before an unbelieving world. Easter faith is
then reduced to "confident belief in certain facts, and a poverty-stricken
hope for the next world, as if death were nothing but a fate we meet . . .
at the end of life," writes Moltmann. "But death is an evil power now, in

---

32. See Sered, *Until We Reckon*, chapter 2; Gilligan, *Violence*, chapters 2, 7; Law, "Prisons Make Us Safer," chapter 2.

33. Moltmann, *Theology of Hope*, 25, 35.

34. Moltmann, *Broad Place*, 100.

35. Moltmann, *Theology of Hope*, 20–21, 35.

36. Moltmann, *Broad Place*, 101.

37. Moltmann, *In the End—the Beginning*, 93. Moltmann, *Theology of Hope*, 23.

life's very midst," that must be challenged.[38] The power of death takes many forms, like the economic death of a family whose basic material needs are not met, the social death of persons locked away in cells, the political death of people we as a society silence or oppress, or the physical death resulting from state-sanctioned violence. As Moltmann argues, the resurrection "is not proved true by means of historical evidence, or only in the next world. It is proved true here and now, through the courage for revolt, the protest against deadly powers, and the self-giving of men and women for the victory of life." Belief in the resurrection is demonstrated "first of all" by "getting up oneself and participating in God's creative power," by "participating in the movement of the Spirit 'who descends on all flesh' to quicken it" (Acts 2:17).[39]

An active and embodied hope recognizes that things are not as they have to be and envisions an alternative future coming to meet us, based on the promises of God. This vision brings people of hope "into contradiction with the existing present," even as it draws them into a deeper love for this life.[40] This leads to the third component of a theology of hope: central to hope is active protest against death's destructive powers. In his remarkable sermon, "Easter: The Festal Protest against Death," Moltmann proclaims, "The Easter faith recognizes that the raising of the crucified Christ from the dead provides the great alternative to this world of death. This faith sees the raising of Christ as God's protest against death, and against all the people who work for death; for the Easter faith recognizes God's passion for the life of the person who is threatened by death and with death."[41] The risen Christ is "God's contradiction" to suffering, evil, and death and the "beginning of God's rebellion" against them. Moltmann writes, "If Paul calls death the 'last enemy' (1 Cor 15:26), then the opposite is also true: that the risen Christ, and with him the resurrection hope, must be declared to be the enemy of death and of a world that puts up with death." God's rebellion continues "in the Spirit of hope, and will be completed when, together with death, 'every rule and every authority and power'" that serves death and carries out its destruction "is at last abolished (1 Cor 15:24)."[42]

---

38. Moltmann, *Power of the Powerless,* 123–124.

39. Moltmann, *Power of the Powerless,* 123–24.

40. Moltmann, *Broad Place,* 103.

41. Moltmann, *Power of the Powerless,* 123.

42. Moltmann, *Theology of Hope,* 21. Moltmann, *Power of the Powerless,* 124.

If Easter is God's protest against death, then resurrection hope "finds living expression" when human beings do the same.[43] Hope turns Christians into "protest people" who cannot align with the status quo but constantly provoke "in order to give shape to the newly dawning possibilities."[44] Whenever faith "develops into hope," the result is "not rest but unrest, not patience but impatience. . . . Those who hope in Christ no longer put up with reality as it is, but begin to suffer under it, to contradict it." Christian communities of hope become "a constant disturbance in human society" and "the source of continual new impulses" toward righteousness and justice on earth.[45] This hope is "unquenchable" until God's work is complete. At the same time, it provides "inexhaustible resources" for the "creative transformation" of society.[46]

But resurrection hope "does not live from this protest."[47] Rather, it stems from a love for life rooted in God—the living God, the Spirit of Life. "Whenever life is threatened," writes Moltmann, "the living God gets involved," for God loves life.[48] While protest alone can too easily dissolve into bitterness, self-righteousness, despair, or resignation, those "seized by the Spirit of the resurrection" have new energies for life despite the negations and "love life without reserve"—not only their own lives but the lives of the neighbor, stranger, or enemy.[49] God is known and experienced through this affirmation of life, not its denial; for God creates life while injustice and violence destroy it. "Human beings are in harmony with God's love for those God has created," says Moltmann, "when they love life, the life of their neighbor, the life they share, and the life of the earth."[50] Moreover, because of the risen Christ, our earthly life now carries eternity within it. "Eternal life is not a different life. It is the resurrection of this life into the life of God," writes Moltmann.[51] As he shared with Kelly, it is this earthly

43. Moltmann, *Power of the Powerless*, 125.

44. Moltmann *Sun of Righteousness*, 77. (Moltmann borrows the term "protest people" from nineteenth-century pastor Christoph Blumhardt.) Moltmann, *Theology of Hope*, 34.

45. Moltmann, *Theology of Hope*, 21–22.

46. Moltmann, *Theology of Hope*, 34. Moltmann, *Broad Place*, 104.

47. Moltmann, *Power of the Powerless*, 125.

48. Moltmann, *Jesus Christ for Today's World*, 23.

49. Moltmann, *Source of Life*, 81. Moltmann, *Sun of Righteousness*, 76.

50. Moltmann, *Living God*, 106, 149.

51. Moltmann, *Jesus Christ for Today's World*, 22.

life that is being raised, healed, restored, and completed. Hope in God, who loves creation and renews the earth, yields this promise: Everything matters. "Nothing will be in vain. It will succeed. In the end all will be well!" Moltmann continues, "We are called to this hope, and the call often sounds like a command—a command to resist death and the powers of death, and a command to love life and cherish it: every life, the life we share, the whole of life."[52]

Perhaps in the abstract, the call to love life may seem fairly uncontroversial and direct. But complications arise for Christians who have been taught to yearn for a better world beyond the grave, since doing so often leads to a diminished view of this earth and our lives in it. Moltmann writes, "It is generally said that life here on earth is nothing but a finite and mortal life. To say this is to allow human life to be dominated by death. But that is then a reduced life."[53] A view that fails to see that eternal life begins now leads to a cheapening of our lives here on earth. This was exemplified in the actions of the Parole Board and the state of Georgia it represents, who lacked reverence for both Kelly's created life and her newly created, restored life. Yet the call to reverence life on earth is not only rooted in God's love for the good creation God made. And it is not only rooted in the possibility of risen life built from the ruins of the past. Love and reverence for earthly life is also rooted in an eschatological promise: the universal and cosmic indwelling of God in all of creation, the promise that God will be "all in all" (1 Cor 15:28).

A fourth component of a theology of hope is that God is utterly committed to earthly life because it is "the stage" of God's eternal dwelling.[54] God is making this earth God's house, God's home, and "all created beings will share this home with him," writes Moltmann as he echoes Revelation 21:3: "Behold the dwelling of God is among mortals. He will dwell with them, and they shall be his people."[55] Moltmann shows that God's mutual indwelling with creation is central to the biblical witness, as seen in the Hebrew concept, *Shekinah*, which he defines as the "indwelling of the Eternal One in history, and of the Infinite One in the finite."[56] *Shekinah* belongs to

52. Moltmann, *Source of Life*, 39.

53. Moltmann, *Living God*, 73.

54. Moltmann, *Sun of Righteousness*, 72.

55. Moltmann, *Jesus Christ for Today's World*, 23. Moltmann, *Sun of Righteousness*, 27.

56. Moltmann, *Sun of Righteousness*, 30.

a theology of hope rooted in the promises of God because it refers to the promise of indwelling, the covenant promise God made with Israel that expands to a universal promise for all people (Exod 29:45), and in the New Testament refers to the indwelling of God in Jesus Christ and the indwelling of the Holy Spirit in bodies and communities, a Spirit that is "poured out on all flesh" (Acts 2:17).

We see God's indwelling from creation onwards, beginning with the act of creation itself. In the creation story in Genesis 2, God's *ruach*—God's spirit—is breathed into the nostrils of the human being and becomes "the breath of life" (Gen 2:7). God creates everything through God's Spirit, writes Moltmann, and, according to Israel's Wisdom literature, every living being has God's Spirit in it. "For you love all things that exist, and detest none of the things you have made," reads the Wisdom of Solomon; "for your immortal spirit is in all things" (11:24, 12:1). This Spirit is, according to the tradition, God's *Sophia*, God's Wisdom. Because God's Spirit is what gives creation life and sustains it, God does not stand wholly outside of creation but has already entered into it.[57] This is not to say that there is no distinction between the Creator and creation. Rather, "the divine and earthly interpenetrate each other mutually: unmingled and undivided."[58] The interpenetration results in "the immanent presence of God in the world in all things."[59] In Israel's Wisdom tradition, the Wisdom with which God created the world is also understood as God's Logos, God's Word, a concept that becomes foundational to the Gospel of John. Referring to Jesus as the incarnate Word, John's Gospel similarly reveals God's immanent presence in all creation: "In the beginning was the Word, and the Word was with God, and the Word was God. . . . All things came into being through him . . . What has come into being in him was life" (John 1:1–4). Or, as Paul writes to the Colossians, "in him all things hold together" (1:17).

Because Jesus is the incarnate Word or Wisdom through which all things were made and hold together, "whoever reverences Christ reverences all created things in him, and discovers him in all created things," writes Moltmann. The inverse is also true: the destruction of human beings created by God is "nothing other than practiced atheism," since human beings, along with the rest of creation, bear the presence of the divine, indeed,

---

57. Moltmann, *Source of Life*, 24. Moltmann, *Sun of Righteousness*, 30–31.

58. Moltmann, *In the End—the Beginning*, 158.

59. Moltmann, *Sun of Righteousness*, 31.

are made in God's image (Gen 1:27).[60] Paul also affirms the indwelling of God in human persons when he tells the Corinthians that their bodies are "a temple of the Holy Spirit," therefore, they should "glorify God" with their bodies (1 Cor 6:19–20). "In saying this," Moltmann writes, "[Paul] is urging Christians to bodily, earthly, social and political obedience to God's commands, in accordance with his righteousness and justice."[61] It stands to reason that we glorify God also by respecting the bodily integrity and protecting the bodily life of others, especially when a temple of the Holy Spirit like Kelly's is threatened. Christians respond to the immanent presence of God in all created persons and things by developing deep reverence for their earthly life and by protecting and sustaining it in anticipation of the day in which the whole earth and everything in it is filled with the glory of God (Isa 6:3). For the earth is becoming the household of God and, we, God's household companions.

An eschatologically minded person—a person of hope—looks to that promised future to know how to live in the present with others here on earth. God's future includes the promise that divine righteousness and justice will fill the earth, making it a new creation, a new earth. A theology of hope defines earthly justice through this lens, namely, as justice that serves the new creation of all things.[62] This understanding of justice is a fifth component of a theology of hope.

Moltmann describes two modes of justice: God's justice "creates" and God's justice "puts right."[63] These modes correlate, respectively, to the needs of victims and perpetrators of harm, recognizing that each of us are, at times and in varying relationships, those who are harmed and those who harm. He turns to the Psalms to understand God's justice from the perspective of victims and argues that any proper understanding of God's justice must begin with them. God "maintains the cause of the afflicted and executes justice for the needy," reads Psalm 140:12. Victims of harm need the *creation* of justice—constructive acts that deliver, heal, and restore and that bring freedom, health, and new life. God's creative justice has what Moltmann calls the "how much more" logic of Paul: "where sin" or harm "increased how much more did grace abound" (Rom 5:20).[64] God's jus-

60. Moltmann, *Sun of Righteousness*, 31–32.

61. Moltmann, *Sun of Righteousness*, 113.

62. Moltmann, *Sun of Righteousness*, 138.

63. Moltmann, *In the End—the Beginning*, 78.

64. Moltmann, *Living God*, 101.

tice, which creates new life where life has been destroyed or diminished, promises to give more to the victim than what was lost—more life in the fullness of God, whether eschatologically or "in the land of the living" (Ps 27:13). While many of us in the West tend to hear a cry for justice as a cry for retribution, even vengeance, Moltmann argues that more often in the Bible the yearning for justice is a cry for personal and communal healing and wholeness. He writes, "In the Old Testament there are ideas about a divine wrath which reacts to human wickedness and punishes the godless; but the prevailing ideas centre on God's creative righteousness and justice. 'Bring about justice for me!' is the appeal to the God who 'creates justice for those who suffer violence.'"[65] The origin of the belief in a judging God comes from victims of injustice who "hope for a judge," who will establish for them communities of justice and peace.

Moltmann connects this cry for justice with the resurrection of Jesus from the dead. On the cross, Jesus is in solidarity with all victims of violence. His sufferings are not his alone but are "inclusive, comprehending the sufferings of all the God-forsaken in this world."[66] Moltmann writes, "If we read the stories about the resurrection with the echo of the Psalms in our ears, we arrive at the idea that the raising of Jesus from the dead has to do with *divine resurrection*, or rising up" on behalf of victims of harm. He observes that the Psalter is filled with the cry for God to arise: "Arise . . . forget not the afflicted" (Ps 10:12); "Bestir thyself and awake for my cause" (Ps 35:23, 44:23); "Arise [and] establish judgment to save all the oppressed of the earth" (Ps 76:9); "Arise, O God, to judge the earth" (Ps 82:8, 108:5). And he concludes, "With the raising of Jesus, God's own 'arising' has begun, and will bring about justice for all the wretched" of the earth. When read through the Psalms, the hope for the resurrection of the dead is not about immortality but is a "hunger" for justice.[67]

When God raises Jesus—the one "who was executed by the power-holders of this world"—God proves that "in the end" the executioners "will not triumph over their victims."[68] The raising of the crucified Christ does not "justify the crucifixion," as members of the Parole Board thought. "It

---

65. Moltmann, *Sun of Righteousness*, 130–31. See also Marshall, *Beyond Retribution*, 40–53.

66. Moltmann, *In the End—the Beginning*, 70.

67. Moltmann, *Sun of Righteousness*, 41.

68. Moltmann, *Broad Place*, 103. Moltmann, *Sun of Righteousness*, 56.

justifies the crucified victim" in the face of "Roman power politics."[69] When Moltmann says in his last letter to Kelly that "those who want to take your life really don't know what they are doing. Forgive them, their future is dark," he is speaking to Kelly as the executed victim and referring to God's judgment on the Parole Board. They are blind to the reality that they are agents of the powers of evil in this world, and they will recover their sight only when they turn to their victim, Kelly, and "learn to see themselves" through her eyes.[70] When they turn to their victim, they will be confronted with the crucified Jesus, who identifies with and takes the side of all of society's victims. Their salvation only comes by way of the crucified and risen Christ, who encounters them "together with their victims."[71]

Moltmann argues that in this way victims and perpetrators are "inextricably entangled," and that God's justice "works on both sides."[72] Perpetrators of harm have to face what they have done and be put on the right road. There they "will receive a justice which transforms and rectifies," writes Moltmann, the "transforming grace" that Paul describes metaphorically as fire (1 Cor 3:15). The fire of God's love "burns away everything which is contrary to God" so that perpetrators of violence may be delivered from the powers of evil they serve.[73] We already witnessed the power of God's transforming justice and love with Kelly, who, as a perpetrator of violence against Doug, faced her role in his murder, remembered her victims, and built from the ruins. In doing so, she prepared the way for, and began to participate in, the creative justice of the new earth. What was possible for Kelly is also possible for those who put her to death, which is why Moltmann exhorts her on the day of her execution to "forgive them." Like the forgiveness Jesus proclaims from the cross—"Father forgive them, for they don't know what they are doing" (Luke 23:34)—Kelly's forgiveness prepares the way for the new earth where God's righteousness and justice will dwell (2 Pet 3:13). "When the victims are raised up and the perpetrators put right, the purpose is not a great reckoning" based on "reward and punishment," writes Moltmann, but the victory of God "over everything godless."[74] The triumph of God's creative justice has nothing to do with separating human

69. Moltmann, *Sun of Righteousness*, 56.
70. Moltmann, *Sun of Righteousness*, 139.
71. Moltmann, *Sun of Righteousness*, 137.
72. Moltmann, *In the End—the Beginning*, 53.
73. Moltmann, *Sun of Righteousness*, 137.
74. Moltmann, *Sun of Righteousness*, 137.

beings into the "saved and damned," since God judges human beings but does not condemn. Instead, God saves condemnation for the powers themselves. Through the condemnation of condemnation, "death will be slain, the power of evil will be dissolved, . . . hell will be destroyed." This "negation of the negative" establishes "the indestructible position of the positive"—God's eternal reign.[75] The purpose of this justice is "God's great day," the eschatological righting of relationships among human beings, who will dwell together with God in the new earth.[76]

There are conditions that correspond with the righteousness and justice of the new earth, that correspond, in other words, with the coming kingdom of God. "These must be promoted," Moltmann writes. "If the kingdom of God is in the process of its 'coming,' correspondences of this kind are then temporal beginnings of that coming and forms of its arrival in time." Human beings anticipate God's kingdom, he says, when we already "allow today something to appear of the new creation which Christ will complete on his day." In other words, anticipations of the kingdom take "practical form" through human action.[77] The sixth component of a theology of hope is this action—constructive work that often includes protest within it.

In relation to Kelly's story, the most obvious condition that corresponds with the kingdom is the abolition of the death penalty. Abolition on the state and federal levels necessitates action by legislators and ordinary citizens alike. Ordinary citizens comprise the will of the people who have the power to elect legislators who are willing to put a bill forward and support that bill through committee hearings and on the house and senate floors. As US Senator and Baptist pastor Raphael Warnock says, voting is a holy act: "A vote is a prayer about the kind of world we want to live in."[78] In death penalty states, the work of ending executions also involves electing district attorneys who will not seek capital punishment, no matter the case. Pressure may be put on legislators through letters and phone calls to representatives, as well as by participating in "lobby days" at State Capitols or in national events like the Annual Fast and Vigil in Washington, DC.[79]

75. Moltmann, *Sun of Righteousness*, 142.

76. Moltmann, *Broad Place*, 104.

77. All quotes in paragraph from Moltmann, *Broad Place*, 104.

78. Warnock, Twitter post, November 16, 2020, 9:06 PM.

79. See http://abolition.org/fastandvigil/index.html.

And resources for the work abound. Up-to-date information about executions and legislation may be found at the Death Penalty Information Center, which has an easily navigable website.[80] The National Coalition to Abolish the Death Penalty, the longest standing coalition dedicated to this work, provides guidance to faith communities who want to engage in political action, like letter-writing campaigns. Bryan Stevenson's Equal Justice Initiative (EJI) provides powerful educational materials connecting death penalty abolition, prison reform, and racial justice—in Montgomery at the Legacy Museum: From Enslavement to Mass Incarceration, and on their website, which includes a list of local organizations in each state with volunteer opportunities.[81] Church communities have an abundance of riches at their disposal to plan grassroots events, like Sunday school classes or adult forums, that may inspire critical reflection and a change of hearts and minds. Christians born to a living hope then anticipate God's kingdom when we join the mobilization efforts of state-wide policy campaigns or support organizations like EJI or the Georgia Resource Center that provide free legal assistance to people on death row.[82]

Christians may also enter the work and anticipate God's kingdom by nurturing mutually transformative relationships with people like Kelly who are directly impacted by the death penalty. Moltmann calls these relationships "open friendship," and he identifies open friendship as a condition that corresponds to the kingdom of God. It is the kind of friendship that some of us in the theology program were able to share with Kelly and the kind of friendship that she and Professor Moltmann formed.

Common views of friendship grow out of ancient Greek philosophy. Plato and Aristotle thought that mutually transformative friendship could only happen between people who shared equal rank or status, and therefore friendship was understood to have an exclusive quality to it. "Jesus breaks through this closed circle of friendship," says Moltmann, by expanding the circle and reducing distance between people who are different. "In the Gospel of Luke," he writes, "Jesus had a name pinned on him as part of a smear campaign; but it actually describes with total accuracy the fellowship he gives to other people: he is called 'The friend of sinners and tax-collectors'

---

80. See https://deathpenaltyinfo.org/facts-and-research/recent-legislative-activity; https://www.ncadp.org/pages/faith-in-action.

81. See www.eji.org. For a list of local organizations, see https://eji.org/get-involved/.

82. See www.garesource.org.

(Luke 7:34)."[83] Jesus recognized their dignity as human beings and did not succumb to societal prejudice. His friendship was simply friendship—companionship and solidarity—"not charitable, condescending help."[84] The friendship practiced by Jesus is "not merely possible" for us, contends Moltmann, but is "also interesting, in a profoundly human sense."[85]

Open friendship may be formed with people incarcerated on death row through letters and visits. Catholic abolitionist Sister Helen Prejean, whose book *Dead Man Walking* sparked a national conversation about the death penalty, offers a detailed guide on best practices for correspondence, including prison regulations to keep in mind so that the letter is received.[86] Over time, letter writing may lead to an in-person visit or regular visitation.

Open friendship may also take the form of relationships with families who have a loved one incarcerated on death row. For example, New Hope House, a house of hospitality in the Catholic Worker tradition, offers hospitality to families during visitation days and scheduled executions.[87] Located in a peaceful spot in the central Georgia woods minutes from death row, New Hope House provides companionship as well as free food, lodging, and transportation to and from the prison. Director Mary Catherine Johnson also accompanies the defendant's family members to death-penalty trials throughout the state, and if they are sentenced to death, works closely with appellate lawyers throughout the lengthy appeals process. Support for families includes genuine care for their loved one, so New Hope House staff and volunteers regularly visit and correspond with many of the men on Georgia's death row.

New Hope House grew out of the work of the Open Door Community, which for decades hosted monthly trips for families traveling from Atlanta to rural prisons hours away. They loaded up church vans and when they arrived families were greeted to an elaborate meal at a local congregation before heading off to visitation. The meals facilitated friendship between members of the church, the Open Door Community, and the families, in turn, providing a network of support. As a result of knowing the men and

83. Moltmann, *Spirit of Life*, 258.

84. Moltmann, "Open Friendship," 31.

85. Moltmann, *Spirit of Life*, 259.

86. See https://www.sisterhelen.org/teenvogue/. See also Georgia Freedom Letters, https://georgiafreedomletters.com.

87. See http://www.newhopehousega.org. See also McBride, *Radical Discipleship*, 253–54.

their families, New Hope House and the Open Door Community part-
nered with organizations around the state that are working to abolish the
death penalty. They exemplify the reality that when the struggle for justice
is grounded in open friendship with people directly impacted by death-
dealing powers, the work becomes personal and more readily sustained.

By "open friendship," Moltmann also means friendship with a public
quality to it—"open affection and public respect" for persons negatively
labeled and marginalized. In this way friendship becomes a "political concept," a public stance and a personal defense of an individual one loves
but society condemns.[88] In Georgia, the public quality of the friendship
is most often seen through vigils that take place on the steps of the State
Capitol every time there is a scheduled execution. Hosted by Georgians for
Alternatives to the Death Penalty, the Open Door, and Central Presbyterian
Church, the vigils serve as both an act of public protest on a visible downtown street and a time for prayer—prayer for the individual, their family,
and the victim's family, as well as for an end to executions. The vigils often
begin with a testimony from someone who has become a friend through
regular visitation. The friend shares about their most recent visit and hu-
manizes the person being executed by introducing them to the crowd in
ways that go well beyond their media image. In this way, we may understand the entire advocacy movement on Kelly's behalf as a full-throttled
expression of open friendship—a public stance and defense of someone we
loved.

Moltmann observes that the open character of Jesus' friendships was
often expressed through feasting, and his motivation for eating and drink-
ing with others was "overflowing joy" in God's approaching kingdom.[89]
"Jesus does not bring a dry sympathy" to his friends but celebrates the
eschatological feast every time they eat and drink. Through this festive
meal, Jesus proclaims that God's kingdom is "present in their midst." The
potluck meals for traveling families at the church had this quality, as leaders like Murphy Davis from the Open Door set the tone with an "inviting
joy."[90] Similarly Mary Catherine Johnson at New Hope House invites joy
as she and others deliver Christmas packages every year to every man on
Georgia's death row. Filled with food, clothes, and toiletries, the packages
are a small yet meaningful gesture that offers "temporary reprieve from

88. Moltmann, *Church in the Power of the Spirit*, 120.

89. Moltmann, *Spirit of Life*, 258.

90. Moltmann, "Open Friendship," 34.

the perennial dark shadow" of prison, in the words of one incarcerated friend, and that ensures Christmas is "not just another day."[91] The vending machine Eucharist Kelly and I shared also had the quality of play around a festive meal. Through it, the visitation room became for us "the wide space of the Spirit" where "both self-trust and trust in one another" could grow.[92] In all these ways, in the joyful presence of God's reign, friends inside and outside prison walls are compelled to "open ourselves and come alive."[93] There, in open friendship, "we sense there is a wide space . . . in which we can expand" and in which evil powers are overcome with good.[94] As Molt-mann says, "Open friendship prepares the ground for a friendlier world."[95]

Preparing the ground for a friendlier world is an apt way to speak about another condition that corresponds with God's kingdom and that is relevant for ending executions: the creation of a culture that isn't punitive. Even once the death penalty is abolished, it can always rear its head again unless we are building a society that rethinks what it means to do justice without condemnation and while reducing harm. A renewed understanding of justice, aligned with the new earth God promises to bring, will not only influence our attitudes about the death penalty but also about the entire prison system. We have seen in a multitude of ways how God's reign counters carceral logic bent on condemnation. As so, it should come as no surprise that the "new thing" God declares through the prophet Isaiah directly implicates prisons: "I am the Lord, I have called you in righteousness, . . . to open the eyes that are blind, to bring out the prisoners from the dungeon, and from the prison those who sit in darkness. . . . See, the former things have come to pass, and new things I now declare; before they spring forth, I tell you them" (Isa 42: 6-9).

In order to anticipate the new thing God is doing—in order to "sing to the Lord a new song" (Isa 42:10)—we need to understand that the death penalty and prisons are connected at their root. They are both death-dealing institutions. They are powers that condemn human beings to death. Fittingly, EJI refers to "life without parole" not as a "life sentence" but more honestly as being "sentenced to die in prison." More broadly, prisons are quite literally killing people; incarceration leads to a lower life expectancy

91. See McBride, *Radical Discipleship*, 80–84.
92. Moltmann, *Spirit of Life*, 259.
93. Moltmann, "Open Friendship," 31.
94. Moltmann, *Spirit of Life*, 255. Moltmann, *Living God*, 139.
95. Moltmann, *Church in the Power of the Spirit*, 121.

for anyone who has done time. The Prison Policy Initiative reports that each year a person spends in prison takes two years off their life expectancy, even once released. Deaths inside the prison are also on the rise from chronic illnesses like cancer as a result of the exceedingly poor healthcare incarcerated persons receive.[96] Likewise, the National Commission on COVID-19 and Criminal Justice found that the rate of COVID deaths in prison are twice as high as the general population.[97] This failure to meaningfully address the COVID-19 pandemic in prisons, jails, and immigration detention facilities reflects what the memorial Mourning Our Losses names as our willingness "to sacrifice the lives of people in confinement."[98] In short, capital punishment, prisons, and the pandemic form part of a social system that makes certain groups of people vulnerable, as Ruth Wilson Gilmore says, "to premature death."[99]

The death penalty and the entire prison system are death-dealing institutions because they engender physical death. They are also principalities of death because they are systems that condemn human beings in the precise way that Jesus denounces when he commands, "Do not condemn" (Luke 6:37). The Mennonite scholar and pioneer of the modern restorative justice movement Howard Zehr uses a term that helpfully describes the condemnation Jesus denounces when he speaks of "disintegrative shame." Zehr draws on a distinction made by Australian criminologist, John Braithwaite, who identifies two kinds of shame, one that condemns the person as bad or evil and one that "denounces the offense but not the offender." The latter, reintegrative shame, may be part of the work of restorative justice in so far as it names a harm that has been done and holds one accountable by offering ways to make things right and restore broken community. But disintegrative shame stigmatizes the person and defines the individual herself as bad, as having little to no moral worth. As Zehr observes, the Western criminal legal system "embodies stigmatizing shame."[100]

When a society defines a person or group of people as having little to no moral worth, it understands freedom as freedom *from* them instead of

96. See https://www.prisonpolicy.org/blog/2017/06/26/life_expectancy/. And https://www.prisonpolicy.org/blog/2020/02/13/prisondeaths/.

97. See https://covid19.counciloncj.org/2020/12/06/impact-report-covid-19-and-prisons/.

98. See https://www.mourningourlosses.org/mission-history.

99. Gilmore, *Golden Gulag*, 28.

100. Zehr, "Restoring Justice," 27.

freedom *for* others. Part 1 argued that the death penalty is the most extreme form of this false freedom; it promotes the idea that we can find freedom as a society by being free from others, in this case, by literally wiping certain people from the face of the earth. But the prison system is also a manifestation of freedom *from* others, in its attempt to master and control by locking a huge portion of the population away in cages and then throwing away the key.

The United States has experienced a 500 percent increase in rates of incarceration over the last forty years. We now have 2.3 million people in prison or jail while seven million are under some form of correctional control. Even our least punitive individual states have higher per capita rates of incarceration than authoritarian nations around the world.[101] Mass incarceration has meant separating people from their families and other social support systems, stripping them of human rights, and exposing them for years on end to violence and trauma at extraordinarily high rates. It has had a ripple effect on friends, neighbors, and families, and especially on children of incarcerated people.[102] All these effects have been concentrated among communities who already face systemic inequality and exclusion; for mass incarceration is a concrete manifestation of racism in Gilmore's sense of "group-differentiated vulnerability to premature death."[103] At the individual level, mass incarceration promotes widespread trauma, and at the social level it is one of the most powerful existing engines of white supremacy.[104] We know that incarceration has a disproportionate effect on poor people of color, that it carries on elements of slavery, Jim Crow, and racial terror by other means, and that it produces and depends on racialized ideas of "criminality."[105] Similarly, we know that racial bias against Black and brown defendants and in favor of white victims influences which cases are capitally prosecuted and who is sentenced to death.[106]

All these factors are entangled with moral discourses that support and mask them. The carceral system depends on the idea that people whom

101. Sawyer and Wagner, "Mass Incarceration."

102. Baranyi et al., "Prevalence of Posttraumatic Stress Disorder." Liem And Kunst, "Post-incarceration Syndrome." Martin, "Impact of Incarceration on Dependent Children."

103. Sawyer and Wagner, "Mass Incarceration." Gilmore, *Golden Gulag*, 28.

104. See Alexander, *New Jim Crow*.

105. See Muhammad, *Condemnation of Blackness*. This paragraph has been drawn from McBride and Fabisiak, "Bonhoeffer's Critique of Morality," 89–90.

106. See https://deathpenaltyinfo.org/policy-issues/race.

we imprison are *deserving* of this treatment—that they deserve to be condemned. The system imposes reductive distinctions between the guilty and innocent, felons and citizens. These distinctions define who people are in the public imagination and shape the most intimate details of their lives for years, in and after imprisonment. Such moral reductionism defies what we know about human beings—that we are complicated and changeable and that none of us can easily be defined by the worst thing we have done. But it also serves an ideological function. If we can reduce justice to locking up "bad people" who have done bad things, then we do not need to deal with the social conditions that led to the harms in question and from which people need deliverance. The moral distinctions that lead us to condemn a person to prison or death row are inevitably racialized, although they can be mobilized without any overt appeal to racism. In an excessively punitive culture like ours, the prison system—fueled by racism and part of the structure of racism—casts a wide net, exposing both people of color and white people like Kelly to condemnation and death.[107]

To begin to imagine human beings as free *for* others awakens us to forms of justice grounded in the responsibility we have for one another and in the interdependence of human life. Such an orientation opposes the foundational lie driving capital punishment and the entire prison system: that we can be free from violence and harm by finding and condemning bad people.[108] It demands instead that we recognize our responsibility for the social order and the lives of others. For, as the Genesis story reminds us, we are each other's keeper.

There are people we can look to and learn from who are already doing the work of creating cultures that practice justice without condemnation. They are finding ways to do justice without state violence and punitive measures. And whether they identify as religious or not, they all share the belief animating Moltmann's theology of hope that "something else is possible."[109] These practices, which have taken on growing importance among those who are working to dismantle the prison system and abolish the death penalty, are often referred to as restorative justice, community accountability, harm reduction, or transformative justice. While our retributive system is

---

107. See Alexander, *New Jim Crow*, chapter 5. See McBride and Fabisiak, "Bonhoeffer's Critique of Morality," 97.

108. See Law, *"Prison Make Us Safer,"* 17–24. See also McBride and Fabisiak, "Bonhoeffer's Critique of Morality," 99.

109. See www.commonjustice.org.

based on the premise that crimes are violations of rules for which people need to be punished, advocates of restorative and transformative justice begin instead from the premise that addressing harms means promoting responsibility and healing. Just as God's justice is relational, creative, and oriented toward the healing of harms and the building of community, so, too, are these paradigms.

The people who are already doing this work include family members of murder victims comprising Journey of Hope. We can learn from their stories of forgiveness, as they share about the impact of restorative justice practices and invite us to join them in seeking productive and constructive responses to violent crime.[110] Led by these families, the aim of Journey of Hope is to abolish the death penalty and provide education about the needs of survivors. The movement includes family members of people incarcerated on death row or executed by the state, since capital punishment also creates victims of violence.

We can learn from the groundbreaking work of Common Justice, an organization that provides a restorative justice alternative to incarceration, rooted in the needs of survivors of violent crime. Common Justice provides accountability without incarceration, especially in relation to serious felonies like assault and robbery. Founder Danielle Sered writes,

> In New York City, we operate the first alternative-to-incarceration and victim-service program in the United States that focuses on violent felonies in adult courts. Locally and nationally, we leverage the lessons from our direct service to transform the justice system through partnerships, advocacy, and by elevating the experience and power of those most impacted. Rigorous and hopeful, we build practical strategies to hold people accountable for harm, break cycles of violence, and secure safety, healing, and justice for survivors and their communities.[111]

Her book, *Until We Reckon: Violence, Mass Incarceration, and the Road to Repair*, shares powerful stories about individuals involved in restorative justice processes. And it argues a key insight: that we cannot end mass incarceration without violence prevention, and we cannot end violence without addressing mass incarceration. Sered shows how the four key drivers of violence—"shame, isolation, exposure to violence, and diminished ability to meet one's economic needs"—are also defining characteristics

110. See www.journeyofhope.org.
111. See www.commonjustice.org.

of incarceration.[112] Arguing that "community is what keeps us safe, not prison," Common Justice cultivates pragmatic strategies and promotes community-based solutions for reducing harm.

The work of Common Justice and organizations like it developed directly out of the activism and consciousness-raising efforts of people experiencing incarceration and of communities of color impacted by state violence.[113] Many of these resources have been collated by organizer and educator Mariame Kaba on transformharm.org, "a resource hub about ending violence." Known for the maxim "hope is a discipline," Kaba says that she wants the materials to foster self-education and be shared within one's communities for the purpose of building something new.[114] Materials range from parenting techniques rooted in restorative justice practices to resources on preventing and responding to gendered violence. The materials are helpful for imagining justice in all kinds of spaces and institutions, be it schools, neighborhoods, religious communities, workplaces, or homes. While the resources offer no simple answers about how to do justice in new ways in each varied space—since it takes practice, a willingness to experiment, courage to take risks and to learn from mistakes—many people are making headway. They are practicing new ways of relating to one another in communities and institutions; studying how these practices are reducing harm, fostering healing, and holding people accountable; and then improving on their practice. Their work testifies to the biblical truth that a new world is dawning.

We can enter this work, too, and create cultures that do not moralize or condemn. What would it look like for us to practice forms of justice *right now* with neighbors, strangers, and enemies that correspond to the new earth God promises to bring and to start *where we are*, in our workplaces and schools, towns and neighborhoods, families and religious communities? Isn't this the kind of justice we want for ourselves: institutional cultures and communal spaces where we feel safe enough, supported and accepted enough, to be able to make mistakes and acknowledge when we are wrong, because we know we won't be stripped of basic relational or material needs? When we have done something wrong, don't we want to have people around us who have the courage to name it and hold us accountable in ways that don't cripple us with shame? Don't we want to feel open and

112. Sered, *Until We Reckon*, 67.
113. See www.incite-national.org.
114. Kaba, *We Do This 'Til We Free Us*, xxv.

free enough to be able to speak honestly with one another, to listen well and be heard? Don't we want opportunities to make things right, repair the harm we have done, and rewrite the scripts about who we are, so that we are not defined by our mistakes? Don't we want people who care about us enough to be committed to us, to remain in community with us as we struggle and grow? And don't we want to be gracious enough and patient enough to be committed to others as they do the same?

We cannot do any of this work alone. After Jesus' crucifixion, the disciples dispersed in devastation and confusion. As Moltmann says, they had lost all hope. Jesus finds them isolated and hiding, as those experiencing devastation are prone to do. He breathes on them and says, "Receive the Holy Spirit," binds them in the power of the Spirit, and sends them out to live in new ways made possible by the resurrection (John 20:19–22). This community, empowered by the resurrection and the Spirit of God, is Jesus' answer to the question he asks Mary as she stands by the tomb devastated and alone: "Woman, why are you weeping?" (John 20:13). Go to the others, he says, and tell them you have seen the resurrected Lord. Moltmann writes of Mary, "She is supposed to find the presence of the risen Christ" in community with others, "as the community of the exalted Lord." Referring to the Spirit's task of birthing communities of hope, he continues, "There is no Pentecost without Easter, that is obvious. But there is no Easter without Pentecost either."[115]

This is the seventh and, for us, the final component of a theology of hope: Hope demands life together in community. The Christian communities that formed "in the multifaith cities of the ancient world" and who were filled with the Spirit of Life "did not come forward as one of numerous religious groups," writes Moltmann. "Instead they acted as a peace-conferring and uniting community of the creator and redeemer of all things. What they wanted was not a new religion but a new world. . . . Their missionary task was not a competitive religious struggle but the peace of the cosmos and the reconciliation of humanity."[116] Likewise, Christians today born to a living hope may partner with other communities of hope, with movements and organizations of every stripe, who are figuring out new ways to do justice without condemnation. Christians born to a living hope may gather together to worship the God of hope; to proclaim to one another the gospel of hope, namely, that a new world has begun; and to invite one

115. Moltmann, *Sun of Righteousness*, 52–53.
116. Moltmann, *Sun of Righteousness*, 68–69.

another to "play your part in the new creation of all things!"[117] In the power of the Spirit and with the energy of the Spirit, we may continuously remind one another that a new world is possible and join forces with others who already know. Nothing is inevitable. Anything is possible, here and now, at the dawn of a new day.

117. Moltmann, *Jesus Christ for Today's World*, 138.

Letters after the Letters:
An Afterword

Dear Jenny,

Congratulations on your new position at McCormick. You are changing from the cornfields of Iowa to the skyscrapers of Chicago, but you will be in a broad theological community.

I can't come to the Bonhoeffer Congress in Basel. We are preparing a symposium for the Korean partners of our theological faculty at Tübingen from the 1st to the 3rd of July. My faculty is celebrating my 90th birthday at Friday July 1, at 14:00. Why don't you come over from Basel?

I am looking forward to reading your book on "Radical Discipleship." I am giving a lecture at the societas ethica in August on my Kelly-Gissendaner-story, death penalty and the spirituality of prisoners.

How good to know that my letters to Kelly are in your hands. I shall send Kelly's letters to you, so that our correspondence is in one hand. I am over 90 years now and must bring my things into a certain order.

Hope to see you again, perhaps in Atlanta in October this year? Take good care of yourself.

  With hope and joy,

    Jürgen

Tübingen, August 1, 2016

Dear Jenny,

Murphy just wrote about closing the Open Door Community. This is sad news. Since their beginning some 35 years ago I used to visit the community every time I was in Atlanta. I heard and saw the true voice of America and a graced community.

I was not able to come to the Bonhoeffer Congress in Basel. So I missed you when you were on this continent. As promised I am sending here Kelly's letters and cards to me since 2010. If you have my letters and cards you have our whole correspondence together.

I am coming to Atlanta October 18–22. Steffen Lösel is organizing a conference in honor of my 90 years. It would be fine to meet with you.

> With love and hope,
> Jürgen

Moltmann and McBride at Emory conference, October 2016.

December 1, 2019

Dear Jürgen,

Advent greetings from Atlanta! I write to share an update on some welcomed changes in my life that have allowed me to finally return to the writing project on Kelly, which will include the correspondence between the two of you.

Last year, on September 1, 2018, the day before my 41st birthday, I married Thomas Fabisiak. Thomas served as the program director of the theology certificate after me and now runs a college degree program inside the prison through a regional liberal arts college called Life University. Many of the women who had taken the theology certificate are now students in the college program. It is a gift to be able to share this work together. In fact, Thomas was present during the advocacy campaign for Kelly, but we only knew each other as acquaintances at the time. I am still on faculty at McCormick Seminary in Chicago and now fly back to Atlanta every weekend. Our home together is a small condo adjacent to where the Open Door Community used to be. It is bittersweet to be so close—a constant reminder of their absence but also a strong feeling that we live on holy ground. I still see many of the men who used to come for meals and services; we often have a chance to greet each other as they walk the gravel alleyway beside our back porch.

Another piece of significant news is that in mid-February, I will begin a discernment process toward ordination in the Atlanta diocese of the Episcopal Church. I had what felt like a textbook experience of calling while at the University of Virginia, over ten years ago. But I do not have a masters of divinity degree, and I could never figure out how to move forward given the demands of an academic job. My marriage to Thomas has opened up much for me: I now have the emotional support to navigate the logistical and financial difficulties of taking this step of discernment and a home in Atlanta that allows me to go through the process here, where we hope to eventually root our lives. The process takes about a year and a half, and while one never knows how these things will go, I am excited to begin this journey. In many ways, since marrying Thomas, I am experiencing a kind of recapitulation, the gathering together and giving back of what seemed lost. I am grateful. And I am holding on to verses in Isaiah 43, read at our wedding and now displayed on our fridge:

> Do not remember the former things;
> or consider the things of old.
> I am about to do a new thing;
> now it springs forth, do you not perceive it?
> I will make a way in the wilderness
> and rivers in the desert.

My intent is not to leave the academy, but I am willing to transition, at least for a season, from the institution of the academy to the institution of the church if need be. I am comforted by the notion that regardless of institutional placement, my vocation remains as a theologian—a lived theologian who hopes to nurture and expand her gifts within the sacramental life of a priest.

All this brings me to Kelly. The trauma of her execution happened at the end of my time in Iowa. McCormick has been a place where I could recover, and I started dating Thomas long-distance six months into my time there. My relationship with Thomas has been healing on many fronts, and now that we are a year into a new stable rhythm of marriage, I have the energy and desire to return to this. I am about to sign a contract with Cascade Books of Wipf and Stock. The book will be small, including an expanded version of an essay on our advocacy for Kelly and your letters.

This summer, I noticed when I placed the letters between you and Kelly in chronological order that some of your letters to Kelly are missing. I already knew that the prison had lost some of her items, like her signed copy of *The Crucified God*. This is part of the dehumanizing character of the prison; the few valued items the incarcerated women have are treated as disposable. I wonder if you, by chance, have copies of the letters you sent Kelly during the second half of 2013 to 2015? I do have the last letter you sent through Steffen.

Finally, I want to thank you for your encouragement to publish these letters and write this story. When Brach Jennings returned a year ago from visiting you for the first time in Tübingen, he relayed your message: "Where is the book on Kelly?" I took that as a loving exhortation to get to it, and I took your words to heart. Please forgive my delay; these letters and this story is a treasure. I am honored to be its custodian.

I am also including two other pieces I've written. One is a reflection after my wedding that I wrote on my honeymoon! The other is a piece that Thomas and I co-wrote together, forthcoming in *Dietrich Bonhoeffer, Theology, and Political Resistance*, edited by Lori Brandt Hale and David Hall (Lexington, 2020). We will be presenting this essay in South Africa in January at the International Bonhoeffer Congress.

With love and gratitude for you, and with well wishes for an expectant Advent,

Jenny

Tübingen, January 25, 2020

Dear Jenny,

Thank you for your long letter of December 1 and your Advent greetings. Sorry for the delay of answering, but I am an old man and forgetful.

Congratulations for your marriage with Thomas. I am sending you my blessings, wishing you lasting love and life-long friendship. Some 70 years ago I met Elisabeth and we fell in love with each other and developed a lasting life-friendship: two theologians as you and Thomas. Elisabeth died three years ago and I am lonely but not alone. She is around me day and night. And our four children are taking good care of me. I am going on with reading and writing, traveling and lecturing (as long as people want to hear me). Since Thomas is working in Arrendale Prison you are working together. That is good. Elisabeth developed her feminist theology and I supported her as much as I could. A marriage between Chicago and Atlanta is difficult, I wish you could come closer together.

Your ordination in the Episcopal Church and your perspective on working in the church: Welcome. I worked as a pastor in the rural village of Wasserhorst for 5 years before I entered the academic world. The work in the congregation is real life, while the air in the academic world is rather thin. So prepare for real life.

I shall never forget Kelly Gissendaner and welcome your book on her. I made no copies of my letters to her, and all her letters are in your hands. She has had a fine hand in painting. Integrate her pictures in your book.

Thank you for the enclosed story of your wedding. I like the words of Isaiah 43.

Thank you also for your piece on Bonhoeffer and the American mass incarceration. It is a scandal in the human world. "White supremacy," would my late friend Jim Cone comment.

Love and Hope to you and you both,
    your friend,

    Jürgen

Bibliography

Aaron, Charlene. "Case for Clemency? Radical Redemption on Death Row." *Christian Broadcasting Network*, March 2015. https://www1.cbn.com/cbnbews/us/2015/march/case-for-clemency-radical-redemption-on-death-row .

Alexander, Michelle. *The New Jim Crow: Mass Incarceration in the Age of Colorblindness.* New York: New, 2010.

Baranyi, Gergo, et al. "Prevalence of Posttraumatic Stress Disorder in Prisoners." *Epidemiologic Reviews* 40 (2018) 134–45.

Beker, J. Christian. *Paul the Apostle: The Triumph of God in Life and Thought.* Philadelphia: Fortress, 1980.

Berkhof, Hendrik. *Christ and the Powers.* Scottdale, PA: Herald, 1977.

Bonhoeffer, Dietrich. *Creation and Fall: A Theological Exposition of Genesis 1–3.* Vol. 3 of *Dietrich Bonhoeffer Works,* 16 vols. Edited by John W. de Gruchy. Translated by Douglas Stephen Bax. Minneapolis: Fortress, 1997.

———. *Discipleship.* Vol. 4 of *Dietrich Bonhoeffer Works,* 16 vols. Edited by Geoffrey B. Kelly and John D. Godsey. Translated by Barbara Green and Reinhard Krauss. Minneapolis: Fortress, 2003.

———. *Letters and Papers from Prison.* Vol. 8 of *Dietrich Bonhoeffer Works,* 16 vols. Edited by John W. de Gruchy. Translated by Isabel Best et al. Minneapolis: Fortress, 2010.

———. *Letters and Papers from Prison.* Translated by Reginald Fuller et al. New York: Touchstone, 1997.

Brock, Rita Nakashima, and Rebecca Ann Parker. *Saving Paradise: How Christianity Traded Love for This World for Crucifixion and Empire.* Boston: Beacon, 2008.

Casey, Susan C., and Lindsay Bennett. "Clemency Application: Application to the Georgia Board of Pardons and Paroles on Behalf of Kelly Gissendaner." https://pap.georgia.gov/pressreleases/2015-02-23/clemency-application-kellygissendaner-available.

———. "Emergency Application for 90-Day Stay of Execution and Reconsideration of Clemency Application." https://pap.georgia.gov/press-releases/2015-03-03/second-gissendaner-clemency-application-available.

Cone, James H. *God of the Oppressed.* Maryknoll, NY: Orbis, 1997.

Cook, David. "The Amazing Grace of Kelly Gissendaner." *Chattanooga Times Free Press,* October 4, 2015. https://www.timesfreepress.com/news/opinion/columns/story/2015/oct/04/amazinggrace-kelly-gissendaner/328626.

———. "The Butterfly in the Death Chamber." *Chattanooga Times Free Press,* March 4, 2015. https://www.timesfreepress.com/news/opinion/columns/story/2015/mar/04/cookbutterfly-georgia-death-chamber/291389/.

Cook, Rhonda. "Former Ga. Chief Justice Regrets Vote in Gissendaner Case." *Atlanta Journal Constitution*, September 2015. https://www.ajc.com/news/local-govt--politics/formerchief-justice-regrets-vote-gissendaner-case/zDuXPyMgqqJH9APKVvC96J/.

———. "Pope: Spare Kelly Gissendaner's Life." *Atlanta Journal Constitution*, September 29, 2015. https://www.ajc.com/news/pope-spare-kelly-gissendaner-life/EDv1HBjOXIQLciQYSJq6WJ/.

Douglass, Frederick. *The Narrative of the Life of Frederick Douglass: An American Slave, Written by Himself.* Edited by John R. McKivigan, Peter P. Hinks, and Heather L. Kaufman. New Haven, CT: Yale University Press, 2016.

Estep, Tyler. "Family of Kelly Gissendaner's Slain Husband: Remember the Victim." *Atlanta Journal Constitution*, September 2015. https://www.ajc.com/news/crime--law/familykelly-gissendaner-slain-husband-remember-the-victim/nk7ECPPboIr7CqO9NkpYhJ/.

Gibson, Camille. "Evil Women Hypothesis." In *Encyclopedia of Women and Crime.* Edited by Frances P. Bernat and Kelly Frailing. August 2019. https://doi.org/10.1002/9781118929803.ewac0106.

Gilligan, James. *Violence: A National Epidemic.* New York: Vintage, 1996.

Gilmore, Ruth Wilson. *Golden Gulag: Prisons, Surplus, Crisis, and Opposition in Globalizing California.* Berkeley, CA: University of California Press, 2007.

Golding, Kim S., and Daniel A. Hughes. *Creating Loving Attachments: Parenting with PACE to Nurture Confidence and Security in the Troubled Child.* London: Jessica Kingsley, 2012.

Griffith, Lee. *The Fall of the Prison: Biblical Perspectives on Prison Abolition.* Eugene, OR: Wipf and Stock, 1999.

Harding, Vincent. *Martin Luther King: The Inconvenient Hero.* Maryknoll, NY: Orbis, 2008.

Hicks, Victoria Loe. "Gissendaner Case Tests the Quality of Mercy." *Atlanta Journal Constitution*, September 2015. https://www.ajc.com/news/state--regional-govt-politics/gissendaner-case-tests-the-quality-mercy/CN5Bol1FZrZSoYLTHfuMVO/.

Hiebert, Theodore. "Retranslating Genesis 1–2: Reconnecting Biblical Thought and Contemporary Experience." The Bible Translator 70 (December 2019) 267–69.

Holland, Melanie M., and Ariane Prohaska. "Gender Effects Across Place: A Multilevel Investigation of Gender, Race/Ethnicity, and Region in Sentencing." *Race and Justice* 11 (2021) 91–112. https://doi.org/10.1177/2153368718767495.

Kaba, Mariame. *We Do This 'Til We Free Us: Abolitionist Organizing and Transforming Justice.* Edited by Tamara K. Nopper. Chicago: Haymarket, 2021.

"Kelly Gissendaner." #KellyOnMyMind. http://www.kellyonmymind.com/videos/.

King, Martin Luther, Jr. *Strength to Love.* Minneapolis: Fortress, 2010.

———. *A Testament of Hope: The Essential Writings and Speeches of Martin Luther King, Jr.* Edited by James M. Washington. San Francisco: Harper and Row, 1986.

Kuruvilla, Carol. "Religious Leaders See Delay as an Act of God." *Huffington Post*, March 3, 2015. https://www.huffpost.com/entry/kelly-gissendaner-execution-delay_n_6794922.

Law, Victoria. *"Prisons Make Us Safer" and 20 Other Myths about Mass Incarceration.* Boston: Beacon, 2021.

Liem, Marieke, and M. Kunst. "Is There a Recognizable Post-incarceration Syndrome among Released 'Lifers'?" *International Journal of Law and Psychiatry* 36 (2013) 333–37.

Marlowe, Jen, and Martina Correia-Davis. *I Am Troy Davis*. Chicago: Haymarket, 2013.

Marshall, Christopher D. *Beyond Retribution: A New Testament Vision for Justice, Crime, and Punishment*. Grand Rapids: Eerdmans, 2001.

Martin, Eric. "Hidden Consequences: The Impact of Incarceration on Dependent Children." *National Institute of Justice Journal* 278 (2017). https://www.nij.gov/journals/278/pages/impact-of-incarceration-on-dependent-childrn.aspx.

Martyn, J. Louis. *Galatians*. Vol. 33A of *The Anchor Bible*. New York: Doubleday, 1997.

———. *Theological Issues in the Letters of Paul*. Nashville: Abingdon, 1997.

McBride, Jennifer M. "Georgia Death Row Inmate Finds Path Back to Hope with 'Costly Grace.'" *CNN Online*, March 2015. https://www.cnn.com/2015/03/06/opinions/mcbridegeorgia-death-row-inmate/index.html.

———. *Radical Discipleship: A Liturgical Politics of the Gospel*. Minneapolis: Fortress, 2017.

McBride, Jennifer M., and Thomas Fabisiak. "Bonhoeffer's Critique of Morality: A Theological Resource for Dismantling Mass Incarceration." In *Dietrich Bonhoeffer, Theology, and Political Resistance*, edited by Lori Brandt Hale and W. David Hall, 89–109. New York: Lexington, 2020.

"A Message from the Children of Kelly and Doug Gissendaner." #KellyOnMyMind. http://www.kellyonmymind.com/children/.

Moltmann, Jürgen. *A Broad Place: An Autobiography*. Translated by Margaret Kohl. Minneapolis: Fortress, 2008.

———. *The Church in the Power of the Spirit: A Contribution to Messianic Ecclesiology*. Translated by Margaret Kohl. Minneapolis: Fortress, 1993.

———. *The Coming of God: Christian Eschatology*. Translated by Margaret Kohl. Minneapolis: Fortress, 2004.

———. *In the End—the Beginning: The Life of Hope*. Translated by Margaret Kohl. Minneapolis: Fortress, 2004.

———. *Jesus Christ for Today's World*. Translated by Margaret Kohl. Minneapolis: Fortress, 1994.

———. *The Living God and the Fullness of Life*. Translated by Margaret Kohl. Louisville: Westminster John Knox, 2015.

———. "Open Friendship: Aristotelian and Christian Concepts of Friendship." In *The Changing Face of Friendship*, edited by Leroy S. Rouner, 29–42. Notre Dame, IN: University of Notre Dame Press, 1994.

———. *The Power of the Powerless: A Word of Liberation for Today*. Translated by Margaret Kohl. San Francisco: Harper and Row, 1983.

———. *The Source of Life: The Holy Spirit and the Theology of Life*. Translated by Margaret Kohl. Minneapolis: Fortress, 1997.

———. *The Spirit of Life: A Universal Affirmation*. Translated by Margaret Kohl. Minneapolis: Fortress, 2001

———. "Sun of Righteousness, Arise! The Freedom of a Christian—then and now—for the Perpetrators and for the Victims of Sin." Unpublished Reformation Day Lecture at Emory University, October 28, 2011.

———. *Sun of Righteousness, Arise! God's Future for Humanity and the Earth*. Translated by Margaret Kohl. Minneapolis: Fortress, 2010.

———. *Theology of Hope*. Translated by James W. Leitch. Minneapolis: Fortress, 1993.

Muhammad, Khalil Gibran. *The Condemnation of Blackness*. Cambridge, MA: Harvard University Press, 2011.

"News Coverage on Kelly's Case." #KellyOnMyMind. http://www.kellyonmymind.com/articles/.

"Nikki's Story." #KellyOnMyMind. http://www.kellyonmymind.com/videos/.

Oppenheimer, Mark. "A Death Row Inmate Finds Common Ground with Theologians." *New York Times,* February 27, 2015. https://www.nytimes.com/2015/02/28/us/a-death-row-inmate-finds-common-ground-with-theologians.html.

Sawyer, Wendy, and Peter Wagner. "Mass Incarceration: The Whole Pie 2020." Prison Policy Initiative, 2020. https://www.prisonpolicy.org/reports/pie2020.html.

Sered, Danielle. *Until We Reckon: Violence, Mass Incarceration, and the Road to Repair.* New York: New, 2019.

"Serious Mental Illness Prevalence in Jails and Prisons." Treatment Advocacy Center (September 2016). http:www.treatmentadvocacycenter.org./component/content/article/220-learn-more-about/3695-serious-mental-illness-prevalence-in-jails-and-prisons-.

Stassen, Glen H. "Biblical Teachings on the Capital Punishment." In *Capital Punishment: A Reader*, edited by Glen H. Stassen, 119–30. Cleveland, OH: Pilgrim, 1998.

"Statement of Kayla Gissendaner, September 19, 2015." #KellyOnMyMind. http://www.kellyonmymind.com/children/.

Stevenson, Bryan. *Just Mercy: A Story of Justice and Redemption.* New York: Spiegel & Grau, 2015.

Ullman, Samuel. "Youth." In *The Silver Treasury, Prose and Verse for Every Mood,* edited by Jane Manner, 323–24. London: Samuel French, 1934.

"Vigil of Light, Life, and Solidarity for Kelly." #KellyOnMyMind. http://www.kellyonmymind.com/videos/.

Weaver, J. Denny. *The Nonviolent Atonement.* Grand Rapids: Eerdmans, 2011.

Williams, Rowan. *A Ray of Darkness: Sermons and Reflections.* Cambridge, MA: Cowley, 1995.

———. *Resurrection: Interpreting the Easter Gospel.* Cleveland, OH: Pilgrim, 2004.

Wink, Walter. *Engaging the Powers: Discernment and Resistance in a World of Domination.* Minneapolis: Fortress, 1992.

———. *Jesus and Nonviolence: A Third Way.* Minneapolis: Fortress, 2003.

Winright, Tobias. "Open Letter to Gov. Nathan Deal Regarding Kelly Gissendaner from a Catholic Theologian." *Catholic Moral Theology* (March 1, 2015). https://catholicmoraltheology.com/open-letter-to-gov-nathan-deal-regarding-kellygissendaner-from-a-catholic-theologian/.

Wright, Robert C. "An Open Letter to Governor Nathan Deal from One Christian to Another." December 2014. https://episcopalatlanta.org/news/bishop-sends-an-open-letter-to-governor-urging-halt-to-all-executions/.

Zehr, Howard. "Restoring Justice." In *Capital Punishment: A Reader*, edited by Glen H. Stassen, 23–33. Cleveland, OH: Pilgrim, 1998.

Ziegler, Philip G. *Militant Grace: The Apocalyptic Turn and the Future of Christian Theology.* Grand Rapids: Baker Academic, 2018.

Letters Cited to Governor Deal and Parole Board

(All professional titles describe author
at the time of the advocacy campaign).

Amesbury, Richard (Chair of Theological Ethics and Director of the Institute for Social Ethics, University of Zurich, Switzerland). Unpublished letter, in the author's possession, 2015.

Bader-Saye, Scott (Academic Dean of the Seminary of the Southwest, Professor of Christian Ethics and Moral Theology). Unpublished letter, in the author's possession, 2015.

Basset, Molly (Assistant Professor of Religious Studies and Director of Graduate Studies, Georgia State University). Unpublished letter, in the author's possession, 2015.

Berlis, Angela (Head of Department for Old Catholic Theology and President of the Swiss Society for Theology, University of Bern, Switzerland). Unpublished letter, in the author's possession, 2015.

Cheng, Mary (National Office of United Methodist Women, PhD in Christian Spirituality from Graduate Theological Union). Unpublished letter, in the author's possession, 2015.

Conley, Aaron (Visiting Assistant Professor of Religious Studies, Regis University). Unpublished letter, in the author's possession, 2015.

Dykstra, Robert C. (Charlotte W. Newcombe Professor of Pastoral Theology, Princeton Theological Seminary). Unpublished letter, in the author's possession, 2015.

Eaton, Elizabeth (Presiding Bishop), Julian Gordy (Bishop of Southeastern Synod), Jessica Crist, (Chair of the Conference of Bishops and Bishop of Great Falls, Montana). Unpublished letter, in the author's possession, 2015.

Faber, Eva-Maria (Rector, Chur University of Theology, Switzerland). Unpublished letter, in the author's possession, 2015.

Feldman-Savelsberg, Pamela (Broom Professor of Social Demography and Anthropology and Director of African and African American Studies Program, Carleton College). Unpublished letter, in the author's possession, 2015.

Gathje, Peter (Associate Dean, Memphis Theological Seminary). Unpublished letter, in the author's possession, 2015.

Lamb, Michael (Faculty of Theology and Religion, University of Oxford). Unpublished letter, in the author's possession, 2015.

Lösel, Steffen (Associate Professor in the Practice of Systematic Theology, Candler School of Theology, Emory University). Unpublished letter, in the author's possession, 2015.

Migliore, Daniel L. (Charles Hodge Professor Emeritus of Systematic Theology, Princeton Theological Seminary). Unpublished letter, in the author's possession, 2015.

Muers, Rachel (Senior Lecturer in Christian Studies, University of Leeds, England). Unpublished letter, in the author's possession, 2015.

Ogi, Eric J. (Masters of Divinity Candidate, Harvard Divinity School). Unpublished letter, in the author's possession, 2015.

Olson, Stanley N. (President, Wartburg Theological Seminary). Unpublished letter, in the author's possession, 2015.

Powell, Karen (Chaplain at Virginia Correctional Center for Women). Unpublished letter, in the author's possession, 2015.

Wilton, Emily (PhD Student, Princeton Theological Seminary). Unpublished letter, in the author's possession, 2015.

Winn, Christian Collins (Professor of Historical and Systematic Theology, Bethel University). Unpublished letter, in the author's possession, 2015.

Ziegler, Philip (Senior Lecturer in Systematic Theology, University of Aberdeen, Scotland). Unpublished letter, in the author's possession, 2015.

Cited Website Resources

Abolition Action Committee—Washington, DC Fast and Vigil
www.abolition.org

Common Justice
www.commonjustice.org

Death Penalty Information Center
www.deathpenaltyinfo.org

Equal Justice Initiative
www.eji.org

Georgia Freedom Letters
www.georgiafreedomletters.com

Georgia Resource Center
www.garesource.org

Incite!
www.incite-national.org

Journey of Hope
www.journeyofhope.org

#KellyOnMyMind
www.kellyonmymind.com

Mourning Our Losses
www.mourningourlosses.org

National Commission on COVID-19 and Criminal Justice
www.covid19.counciloncj.org

National Council to Abolish the Death Penalty
www.ncadp.org

New Hope House
www.newhopehousega.org

Prison Policy Initiative
www.prisonpolicy.org

Sister Helen's Ministry Against the Death Penalty
www.sisterhelen.org

Made in the USA
Monee, IL
14 July 2022

99647773R00118